Testimonials for Get Your Kink On

"*Rarely does one come across a book simultaneously packed with such valuable knowledge and delightfully wicked humor.* Get Your Kink On *is that book. Flipping on its head the common trope that intimacy and erotic passion cannot coexist, it illuminates deep truths about the intersection of love and lust, common roadblocks life and marriage throw up, and basic and next level lessons in playtime for grown-ups that make for a potentially life-changing read.*

It's liberating yet respectful, fun yet heartfelt, edgy yet wholly accessible. Get Your Kink On *is not just a timely, practical, and comprehensive guide to getting your kink on (though it is definitely that). It's superpower is in giving readers permission to explore and embrace the most hidden sides of themselves—the scariest, wildest, most debauched yet inhibited parts they (ironically) most want to touch, reveal, and share with their lover or spouse.*"

—Kristin "K.C." Casey
Certified Sexuality Counselor &
IPSA trained Sexual Surrogate
Author of *Rock Monster: My Life with Joe Walsh*,

"*I found this book very entertaining. The author introduces the concept of Imaginative Relaxation which can place the reader into an imaginative state. This makes reading the book a wild ride into quasi fantastical sexual experiences even though he is presenting us with facts. Recommended reading, but not for the faint-hearted.*"

—Alfred Bellanti
Certified Hypnotherapist
NLP Master Practitioner

"As an emergency room physician, I see people come through that suffer sex and kink gone wrong. Viagra overdoses, cock rings that won't come off, the suffering shakled with no key, dildoes and other items stuck deep in the rectum . . . so for those who want to particiate in kink, swinging, and BDSM safely and responsibly this book is a must."

—Dr. Amy Montgomery

"I wasn't sure what to expect when this book was suggested to me by a trusted colleague. Dr. Edgette has managed to provide an extremely detailed explanation of ways to support clients who are facing intimate concerns. As a practitioner, this handbook is a perfect resource. It's extremely valuable for anyone who works with clients related to sexual issues because the author gets to the heart of the matter without ignoring real-life issues. Speaking not as a practitioner, but as a human, this book also helps explore a variety of fascinating sexual experiences in a titillating manner. Freedom to express sexual desires is a much-needed topic and Dr. Edgette is the one to encourage. I highly recommend this book!"

—Patti Sapp,
Hypnotherapist,
Author & Tree Hugger

Get Your Kink On

Get Your Kink On

Dos and Don'ts of Sexual Exploration

Dr. J. H. Edgette

John@edgettetherapy.com

Other books
by Dr. J. H. Edgette:

The Handbook of Hypnotic Phenomena in
Psychotherapy (with J.S. Edgette)

Winning the Mind Game: Hypnosis and
Sport Psychology (with Tim Rowan)

Hypnotic Erotic: A Practitioners Guide to
Sexual Healing

Psych Horse Handicapping: Using Your Head to Win by a Head
and Be Ahead)

About the Author

Dr. J. H. Edgette received his doctoral degree in clinical psychology in 1985 from Hahnemann Medical College and Graduate School in Philadelphia, PA. He has practiced as a psychotherapist for over thirty years in agencies, clinics, group practices, and private practice. He has been licensed as a clinical psychologist in Iowa, Illinois, and Pennsylvania.

He now practices as a sexologist, life coach, and changeologist. He is the author of four books, three edited volumes, and over seven journal articles. His works have been translated into seven languages. He has been asked to give keynote addresses and seminars at over fifty professional conferences and has taught in over thirty states and fifteen countries around the world.

As America's foremost "sexpert," Dr. Edgette is the first doctor of clinical psychology to affirm that kink, fetish, BDSM, Dom/sub, and swinging can be healthy for couples, and even enhance intimacy in relationships.

As a LGBTQ++ friendly and sex-positive feminist, he is prominently listed in the directory "Kink Aware Professionals" which is hosted by The National Coalition for Sexual Freedom.

Dr. J. H. Edgette is available to practitioners via zoom or Facetime for individual consultation and/or advice regarding clients with sexuality or other issues. He is also available for sessions with individuals having issues with sexuality or a variety of other problems.

For more information call, text, email, or Facetime him at 917-806-1850 or at john@edgettetherapy.com

A request to the reader:

I am a sexologist, a psychologist, and a changeologist. I very closely observe people in all sorts of sexual situations. *No one should assume that just because I know a lot about a certain sexual predilection that I engage in it.* On the other hand, *don't ever assume I don't.* So, too, for the ones I love and have loved.

Dedication:

To the Catholic Church for creating strict, harsh, and guilt-inducing taboos. You have made sex so fucking good!

Table of Contents

PART ONE:

FOREPLAY

CHAPTER 1

So You Want
To Get Your Kink On?

G*et Your Kink On* is the first book by either a psychologist or physician to explicitly advocate common but previously secretive and clandestine erotic activities such as BDSM, swinging, kink, and Dom/sub play as not only healthy and fun, but also as contributing to the closeness of the couple. This is also the first book to utilize the power of Imaginative Relaxation (IR) to enhance and expand erotic sexuality.

Since this book provides the key of Imaginative Relaxation to unlock a person's most erotic, yet self-inhibited, repressed, or undiscovered kinky desires, such that they are then set free to roam the conscious mind. Originally residing in the unconscious mind, these dirty desires await hedonic opportunities to see the light of day. Imaginative Relaxation is the best tool for accessing the unconscious and then mining these untapped dirty diamonds of lust.

By expressly normalizing consensual kink *Mating* gives permission for individuals to let these impure impulses be discovered and then see the light of day (or night). Practical and prescriptive, this book will take the reader from envying the men and women in *Sex & the City* and *Fifty Shades* to actually sensibly implementing, in a step-by-step way, these desires with consenting adults.

While liberating, this book does not advocate a sexual free-for-all for readers but instead respects individual differences and desired limitations and constraints. Also, activities need to be safe, sane, and consensual.

Other psychologists and sex therapists render themselves irrelevantly vanilla in recommending the hokey ideas of the occasional (yes, they will insist it be occasional or else they will label you pathological) blindfold, French maids outfit, or having sex on the kitchen table. I unabashedly use my full authority as a psychologist to endorse, on a case-by-case basis, the full exploration of one's most erotic desires.

In summary, I write this book because, while in private lives and public media a fascination and interest in kink abounds, most people don't know how to get in touch with their most erotic self or feel too guilty or inhibited to develop these secret growing predilections. *Mating* contains the key to helping the reader discover and then get comfortable with that which they want to do. Then it guides the actualizing and enacting of the preferred play way. So read on and then get your kink on!

CHAPTER 2

Lust and The Family

Sex, one of the most exciting things in the world, can become damn boring or even irrelevant over time. Why should this be? We start our relationships with frothy erotic fun. We experiment. We do things we've never done before. Our partners different experiences lead us to try things that they have done but we have not. All in all these are lusty days, and couples typically cannot wait to get their hands on each other.

So why should this come to an end? I have identified five formidable factors that almost inevitably lead to much less sex, less exciting sex, and overall boredom in the bedroom. These five fuck-less factors include, but are not necessarily limited to, habituation, familiarity, routine, babies and young children, and work demands. Any one of these can put a damper on one's sex life. Yet they usually happen in some combination. If we were unfortunate enough to have all five factors happen at once, what we would have would be coming home to a partner we do not really see because we see them all the time, the very same partner we are always with, an unvarying routine of undressing your partner in the same way, kissing for the same length of time, and then a predictable sequence of breast touching, genital stimulation, perhaps some sucking, followed by the usual length of what has now become intercourse instead of fucking. Top that off with the baby crying or a young child knocking at the bedroom door and an overdue and important work project, and what you have is an utterly boring or even a nonexistent sex life.

In and of themselves these things are developmentally and evolutionarily adaptive. We bond with one person for long periods of time in order to form the safety and security needed for family life. By definition this winds up being the same person every night, all the time. We naturally have the tendency to get lazy and uncreative in bed over time, resulting in a sickeningly sameness of sequences. Then, in addition, in this developmental stage in the family lifecycle, babies and young children need to be prioritized. Moreover, monies need to be generated to ensure safety, security, and survival.

It's not as if any of these things are unusual or pathological in and of themselves. Quite the contrary. They are normal and needed biological, developmental, and evolutionarily necessary events. The problem occurs when couples go through this time and forget the fun they once had. They begin to lead parallel lives and when the children get older and work situations become more secure they don't seek to recapture the rapture and the erotic excitement that they once had. Sometimes they just let the boredom go on. For others they begin to seek the pleasures they once had with each other by having an affair, going for massages with "happy endings," or becoming overly enamored with ever increasing amounts of internet porn.

There is another different, but complementary, way of saying all this. Marriage and the simplicity of monogamy that come with it are ideal for child rearing and for the economic viability of the family. It thrives in an atmosphere containing love. Yet this love should never be confused with either romantic love or lust/ love. These loves sometimes co-exist, but most often not. This book is designed to maximize the possibility of all loves living in harmony in a domesticated and civilized "wild."

The good news is that all the deleterious tendencies can be undone and overcome with Imaginative Relaxation. Even more encouraging is the fact that Imaginative Relaxation can help a couple to even go way beyond the fun they had when they first met. The exploration of lusty options can and should be a lifelong event.

Imaginative Relaxation can accomplish this in innumerable ways. For example, in age regression a person can be reminded of the fun that they once had. In future progression they can envision and try on for size possibilities that they may want to make eventualities. They can get in touch with erotic and libidinal urges that they never even knew that they had but discover in their sleep when they have an Imaginative Relaxation wet dream. These are just a couple of the ways in which Imaginative Relaxation can help individuals and couples to regain and recapture a sexual energy, interest, and vigor. A quick glance at the table of contents for this book gives an indication of how there are many additional ways that Imaginative Relaxation can contribute to the reestablishment of a healthy sex life. IR can enliven a couples sex life after the biological and developmental demands of early family life have passed, and give them ideas of how to have sex fun in the meantime.

The remainder of this book will be largely devoted to delineating all the ways in which trance can trigger an erotic revolution. First though, two more preliminary or "foreplay" chapters become necessary. The initial one teaches you how to put yourself or client into a Imaginative Relaxation state by illustrating various inductions. The next foreplay chapter teaches you how to develop the proper mental attitude for giving yourself or client Imaginative Relaxation suggestions. This is a much underappreciated yet vital aspect of successful IR work. Too often Imaginative Relaxation suggestions are thought of as mere statements that are given in a mundane fashion once induction has taken place. Nothing can be further from the truth, as you'll see in that chapter. Read on so you can get it on and get on with it.

CHAPTER 3

What's Love Got To Do
With It? Plenty!

Why mate in the wild? Well, it has nothing to do with public sex! Although it could. Just not necessarily. Read on.

It is a horrid notion that good love means being in captivity. How insulting to good relationships! The "mating in captivity" contingent would have it that you escape from the confining boredom of togetherness by role-playing and other methods (invariably vanilla) that provide emotional distance and unfamiliarity, such that it all feels fresh, new, novel, and attractive upon your return to your designated cage. The thought is that you are temporarily freed from the confines of commitment by these games and therefore can afterward stand going back to the tedium, drudgery, and sameness of your union. And have good sex without abandoning love.

It's different from all that, and that is what "getting your kink on" represents. Here it is the very love of the partner and their love for you that allows a couple to be brave enough to engage in voracious debauchery. Intimacy is then liberating and not a limitation you are trying to get past to have hot sex. Closeness gives the couple the very security that allows them to engage in all sorts of super sizzling sex. Caring and closeness is not something you have to work around in order to once again be on fire for each other, it is the very thing that allows you to feel safe enough to venture forth into the wild of swinging, BDSM, Dom/sub, fetish, kink, and the like. And afterward, you feel *more* love and intimacy toward your mate. Why? Because you are partners in crime, having remained emotionally close after deciding together to break a taboo and then breaking it.

It is not about being able to better tolerate the old grind. Love allows for greater freedom to explore while feeling secure. And of course exploring in a vanilla fashion is not the antidote to relationship atrophy.

Keep in mind that those feelings of tender sweet love are temporarily suspended while venturing into the "wild." Love really has nothing to do with hot sex apart from enabling it to happen and also providing for a soft landing afterward. On a landing pad that has been upgraded while you were out playing. To feel love as you are getting your kink on will just spoil and delimit the pleasure of erupting lust. But boy is love better and deeper afterward.

As partners in crime you will laugh together and reminisce and recount your adventures during sex for weeks or months to come.

Okay, now the "Foreplay" experience is heightening! Read further to learn how to get into the state of mind called "Imaginative Relaxation" and how to use it to become the kinkster you have always wanted to be!

CHAPTER 4

Imaginative Relaxation: The Foundation of Wish Fulfillment

In order for anything to happen, that you want to happen, in the chapters that are about to happen, you need to make deep relaxation happen. We will get to the imaginative part later but for now understand that relaxation is the foundation upon which you wish wishes and upon which they then come true. It is the fertile soil upon which you softly plant the seed of a hope. Then repeating this cycle over a few days provides the sunshine and water needed for the plant of intended new lust to grow and flourish. More on this Imaginative intentionality later, for now it is time to relax.

Deep relaxation creates a state like, and is as powerful as, meditation, yoga, being in the zone, contemplative prayer and so on. It is a peak experience, can become a plateau experience, and tends to have a spiritual flavor.

Can't relax you say? SHUT UUUUUPPP! Everyone has a long history of at least intermittent *deep* relaxation. You claim you don't remember? Here, let me remind you of what you don't know that you know. Your subconscious is where your memories reside and all you need to do is tickle it to open up a treasure trove of vivid memories of relaxation. So if one of the following releases a thread of a memory, pull on it gently. Go with it, make it vivid. Very vivid. Make it sensory. Very sensory. Sight, sounds, smells, tastes and touch blossom, yet in a refined way.

Surely you can remember some of these . . . . . .

- Laying on the beach
- Gently swinging in a hammock
- Gazing out at a magnificent vista such as the Grand Canyon or a mountain range
- Hiking on a trail in a forest.
- Listening to Gregorian chants
- When you first held your baby and went into a revery of gentle, soft gazing
- Daydreaming on a long easy car ride
- Sitting alone in one of the world's great cathedrals . . . .
- A long relaxed jog
- Practising your meditation and transcending
- Looking at beautiful art in an empty museum

- Feeling centered and gently focused immersed in a sweet and sublime yoga session
- Reflecting back on a hypnosis session you once had

These should all be developed and enriched with deep vivid sensory stimuli. One of the reasons for this is that that approach facilitates the experience of relaxation. It is no longer conceptual but sensory, and the mind responds accordingly. Another way of putting this is that anything the mind remembers vividly and in a sensory fashion becomes real once again.

Here are a couple of examples of how it might look. You would think to yourself . . . .

" I am on the beach, just arrived. I lay down on a soft lounge chair with a thick terry cloth towel underneath me. I run one hand down the side of the towel immersing myself in the texture. My other hand goes into the sand and rolls the grains between my fingers. I am getting ever more relaxed. I focus so it is like this is the only thing that exists, the outside world with its stressors fades away. Waves lap. Saltwater air. Seagull soars and sounds. Kids play ball. Radio rock. Ice cream jingle man calls out. More and more relaxed.

Get the idea? Here is another . . . ..

"Chartres, stained glass, coloured glass, soar, saints, saints, saints, candles candles, candles, once mom said 'don't stare at candles in church, you will become hypnotised' but I want that. Relax. The deafening sound of silence. Old smells, incense smells, can kneel, don't kneel, old wood stroke with hand. Relax relax, relax.

One person walk, heels. Echo, echo, echo, click click, click stop. Church bell church bells, church bells, noon, hungry. Outside air fresh. Souvenirs to buy. Lady old kerchief vail wrinkle face. Jambon, gruyere, baguette, Evian. Bus drives away. Chartres in looms outstanding in its field. Smile and Sigh"

Do this for whichever scenarios you choose, mine or yours. Keep making them more and more vivid and you will build a solid foundation of relaxation. Upon that rock, you will build an attitudinal stance that is optimal for sexual wishes, or any wishes for that matter, to come to fruition. This excellent orientation, the one that allows the wishes to come to life, is the topic of the next chapter.

CHAPTER 5

The Art of Giving Self Suggestion: How to Wish a Wish

Imaginative Relaxation can be used with both adults and children. When the topic of giving oneself suggestions in Imaginative Relaxation is addressed it is almost always as if it is simply a matter of saying words to oneself once the induction has been completed. That approach limits the potential for effective self suggestion because it frames the change intervention as being linguistic and technical only. Having the proper mental stance or attitudinal position is at least as important as the words themselves.

I propose a set of illustrative metaphors that will enable the practitioner of Imaginative Relaxation to adopt an optimal psychological position vis-à-vis the suggestion being given such that it has maximum effect.

These metaphors harken to times in the past where the optimal mental attitude was present. As such, they provide a historical reference point and resource for the practitioner of self Imaginative Relaxation such that they can easily adopt the proper psychological position that will enable the desired suggestion to have maximum impact.

Please note that these illustrative metaphors are appropriate for all but the most stodgy adults. That is to say, no doubt there are some CPAs, engineers, and surgeons, who will balk at their playful and often regressive nature. Nonetheless, for most, they will serve as an ideal template with which to understand that which is meant by an optimal mental attitude or stance.

Self suggestions are best conceived as personal wishes embedded in an optimal psychological framework. The wish alone is not enough, it must be put forth coming out of the right attitude that will enable the self to organize such that the wishes befor filled.

Once the self, especially the subconscious mind, adopts the proper stance it will work "behind the scenes" and "run in the background" to scan the environment for opportunity to actualize the wish. This is also what the "law of attraction" is about.

The following metaphors will quickly serve to show subjects the correct way to wish their Imaginative Relaxation wishes:

- "Everyone has had the experience of being presented with a birthday cake with candles on it. Your task then becomes taking a moment and making a wish for something to come true while then seeking to blow out all the candles such that it does."

— "Many of us have seen a shooting star in the night sky. When we do we quickly make a wish in the hopes that viewing this phenomena will allow it to come true."

— "More commonly, all of us have seen the first star in the night sky. At that moment we take the opportunity to offer up a wish that we hope will take place."

— "On Thanksgiving day it is common for a dried out turkey wishbone to be grabbed at each end by two small children who each pull. The one who gets the bigger piece either makes a wish on the spot, which he/she hopes to come true, or hopes that the wish that he made prior to the contest comes to fruition."

— "Just about every one of us has had the opportunity to throw a coin into a fountain or a pool of water. Prior to tossing the coin you make a wish and then upon tossing gently hope that it will come true."

These metaphors are common everyday examples, many from childhood, that adeptly illustrate the optimal mental approach or attitude to giving oneself wishes or self suggestions. That most of them require something to change in the world at large is beside the point. We all secretly recognize that what we are hoping for is some shift in conscious or subconscious functioning such that the environment reacts differently to us and our wish comes to fruition. Again, it is the law of attraction.

It is important to recognise that both IR and self suggestion can be used by yourself to yourself or by another person helping you. It is ideal for couples facilitating each other's sexual liberation.

Please note that some of these metaphors may be culturally bound. Obviously, if the metaphor is not found in a particular culture it makes little sense to use it, unless you are enchanting a person with possibilities that exist in other cultures.

When working in non-North American cultures it can be interesting and useful to find out the contexts within which wishes there are seen to actualize. I can remember asking about this while teaching in Russia. There were many very interesting and unique examples of times when wishes might most easily come to fruition. One that comes to mind concerns the notion that if a person is standing between two people of the same name it is lucky. Therefore, it is a superb time to make a wish for something you want to come true. That is to say if you have a man named Andre on your right and another man named Andre on your left you have satisfied the conditions for good fortune with regard to any wish made.

It is my hope that this approach to making self suggestion will increase the effectiveness of these wishes for change. Such is been my experience in clinical practice and I think it makes good clinical sense that Imaginative Relaxation suggestions to oneself or another should be more than just a set of words introduced after an induction.

The specific sexual wishes themselves, and how you know which ones you want to come true, will provide the content of the rest of the chapters.

PART TWO

KINKSTER TRAINING

CHAPTER 6

What Flavor of Kink
Do You Want?

So you want to get kinky? Well you probably aren't reading this if you don't already have something in mind! But don't stop with the flavor of kink you already know turns you on. There are flavors you have not tried, ones you have not ever seriously considered, and ones you didn't even realize exist!

First, know that whatever kink you have on your mind will likely evolve. Pervy preferences tend to become ever more specific and differentiate. It is like a tree trunk sprouting branches and then those branches in turn sprout branches, and so on. For example, a foot fetish may go from general worship of feet that only have a nice pedicure to feet in leather sandals to feet in heels showing a lot of "toe cleavage."

Second, know that you are likely to switch off or have parallel kinks at some point. You may surprise yourself at what you like that you did not know that you liked. For example, I once worked with a woman who liked public exhibitionism and thought that that was the whole shabang for her. One night at a swingers club her husband deemed her acting like a "brat" for being outright rude to an interested man. He half jokingly said she should be spanked for her behavior. She playfully dared him, while bending over and pulling up her skirt leaving her panty less butt in the air. He took her up on the offer and they got into some serious BDSM role play. "Master Keye" taught "Brat Nicole" a lesson. In session with me she blushingly confessed, "As a senior Vice President with an Ivy League graduate degree in finance I AM SO VERY EMBARRASSED AT HOW MUCH I LIKE TO BE SPANKED!"

Third, if you are unsure of your preferred kink there are a couple of good ways to find out which ones will be your fave. One way is to take seriously what turns you on and off in erotica. Another way is to see what scenes you like in sexual TV shows and movies. The best way to get your kink on however is to attend closely to the fantasies that build up to your orgasm when masterbating. Pay particular attention to the fantasy that you like to cum to. Take that most seriously. That is what you crave, what you hunger for.

Forth, an excellent way to figure out either what particular pervy pleasure turns you on or how far you want to go in a given sexual direction is to use Imaginative Relaxation. Go into the IR relaxed state, manifest a successful wish mind set, and envision yourself in various potential scenarios. You will be able to tell by your response, during and after, what flavor brand and amount is right for you. Given a Baskin Robbins 28 Flavor world of kink you will have plenty of fun sorting to do.

To get a sense of all the possibilities for kink, fetish, BDSM, and Dom/sub you can sample the offerings of one of the many kink fests held around the world. One of the most famous is the "TES Fest" which is held almost every year over the July 4th weekend. The venue is typically a brand name hotel in north New Jersey, bought out in advance ("hotel takeover"), so that everyone can walk around in their favorite fetish garb non-stop all weekend long.

On the next page are the workshop and event choices from 2019. You will see that you can sample the fare Chinese restaurant style; that is, one from column A, one from column B, one from column C, and etc. Another way of thinking about it is to imagine that you are sampling new flavors of ice cream with those little taste-test spoons.

TES Fest 2019

Thursday, July 4

Salon A

2:00 p.m. - 3:00 p.m. – Sexy, Safe and Pain-free Anal

3:30 p.m. - 5:00 p.m. – Points of Interest

5:30 p.m. – 6:30 p.m. – The Corset Class . . . How and Where to Buy, How to Tie And How to Correctly Wear a Corset!

Salon B

2:00 p.m. - 3:00 p.m. – Strap-On For All Gender Identities

3:30 p.m. - 5:00 p.m. – Doll Play

5:30 p.m. – 6:30 p.m. – Fetiquette

Salon C

2:00 p.m. - 3:00 p.m. – Going Primal- RRAWWR!!

3:30 p.m. - 5:00 p.m. – Rope 102 Harnesses and Hog Ties

5:30 p.m. – 6:30 p.m. – Beyond the Kitchen Table: Modes and Models of Parallel Polyamory

Salon D

2:00 p.m. - 3:00 p.m. – Risk Assessment For Masters

3:30 p.m. - 5:00 p.m. – Sensual Steel: The Art of Erotic Knifeplay

5:30 p.m. – 6:30 p.m. – Fucking With Gender

Salon E

2:00 p.m. - 3:00 p.m. – Mental Health and Kink

3:30 p.m. - 5:00 p.m. – Unequal Partnerships: A Collaborative Model of Dominance/submission

5:30 p.m. – 6:30 p.m. – Geezers and Groaners: Aging and Disabilities in Master/slave Relationships

Boardroom A

2:00 p.m. - 3:00 p.m. – Kinky Creativity

3:30 p.m. - 5:00 p.m. – Sissification For Newbies

5:30 p.m. – 6:30 p.m. – Femdom: Finding Your Feminine Leadership Style

Boardroom B

2:00 p.m. - 3:00 p.m. – The Beauty of Objectification

Dungeon

Opens for play at 8:00 p.m.

Courtyard

8:00 p.m. – 9:00 p.m. – Special Event: LGBTQ+ Meet & Greet

9:00 p.m. – 10:00 p.m. – Special Event: Novice and Newcomers

Pool

9:00 p.m. – 12:00 a.m. – Special Event: Pool Party

Restaurant

10:00 p.m. – 11:00 p.m. – Special Event: Queer

Friday, July 5

Salon A

9:00 a.m. – 10:30 a.m. - Art of Erotic Healing

11:00 a.m. – 12:00 p.m. - Wax Play-Artistic, Sadistic, and Cheaptastic

1:00 p.m. – 2:30 p.m. – Intro to Needles

3:00 p.m. – 4:00 p.m. – Putting a Fine Point On It: Pressure Points for Kink

4:30 p.m. – 5:30 p.m. – Breathplay 101: Just the Basics

6:00 p.m. – 7:00 p.m. – Violet Wand Play

8:00 p.m. – 4:00 a.m. – Dungeon Open for Play

Salon B

9:00 a.m. – 10:30 a.m. - Art of Erotic Healing

11:00 a.m. – 12:00 p.m. – Ownership 101

1:00 p.m. – 2:30 p.m. – Get Switchy With It: Navigating Play Dynamics As a Switch

3:00 p.m. – 4:00 p.m. – Kidnapping Without the Jail Time

4:30 p.m. – 5:30 p.m. – Building a Better Kit

6:00 p.m. – 7:00 p.m. – Non-monogamy and the Law

8:00 p.m. – 9:00 p.m. - Dungeon Open for Play

Salon C

9:00 a.m. – 10:30 a.m. – Heavy Duty: Suspending Larger People

11:00 a.m. – 12:00 p.m. – Emotional Edgeplay

1:00 p.m. – 2:30 p.m. – Techniques for Play with a Singletail

3:00 p.m. – 4:00 p.m. – The Far End of M/s: Consensual Non-consent, TPE, and Internal Enslavement

4:30 p.m. – 5:30 p.m. – Erotic Wrestling

6:00 p.m. – 7:00 p.m. – Intro to Sadistic Rope

8:00 p.m. – 9:00 p.m. - Dungeon Open for Play

Salon D

9:00 a.m. – 10:30 a.m. – Communicating Risk: Creating Informed Consent

11:00 a.m. – 12:00 p.m. – Not So Random Acts of Sadism

1:00 p.m. – 2:30 p.m. – Ritual Binding

3:00 p.m. – 4:00 p.m. – Flogging 101: Boymeat Can Flog, So Can You!

4:30 p.m. – 5:30 p.m. – Woven Harnesses

6:00 p.m. – 7:00 p.m. – Power, Surrender, & Safety: Negotiating Unequal Relationships When You're Gender Transgressive

8:00 p.m. – 9:00 p.m. - Dungeon Open for Play

Salon E

9:00 a.m. – 10:30 a.m. – Using Hypnosis to Control Arousal, Orgasms, and Chastity

11:00 a.m. – 12:00 p.m. – Negotiating While Fractionated

1:00 p.m. – 2:30 p.m. – Interrogation

3:00 p.m. – 4:00 p.m. – Introduction to Erotic Hypnosis

4:30 p.m. – 5:30 p.m. – Atmosphere, Mood, and Tone

6:00 p.m. – 7:00 p.m. – Hypnosis for Non Hypno Fetishists

8:00 p.m. – 9:00 p.m. – Special Event: Dominant Ladies Meet and Greet

10:00 p.m.—11:00 p.m. – Special Event: Hypno Lounge

Boardroom A

9:00 a.m. – 10:30 a.m. – Volunteer Orientation

11:00 a.m. – 12:00 p.m. – Polyamory and Power Exchange Relationships

1:00 p.m. – 2:30 p.m. – High Protocol: Verbal Restrictions and Positions

CORRECTED BELOW

3:00 p.m. – 4:00 p.m. – Bottom of the Slash 101 in 24/7 Life

4:30 p.m. – 5:30 p.m. – Rope Bottoming 101

6:00 p.m. – 7:00 p.m. – Using Your Voice in Master/slave Relationships

Boardroom B

11:00 a.m. – 12:00 p.m. – Blood Choking 101

1:00 p.m. – 2:30 p.m. – Aria's Sing Along

3:00 p.m. – 4:00 p.m. – The Halo Above Your Heart: Collars and Collaring

4:30 p.m. – 5:30 p.m. – Introduction to Facial Torture

6:00 p.m. – 7:00 p.m. – Comedy Condoms

9:00 p.m. – 10:00 p.m. – Special Event: Introvert Recharge

Courtyard

3:00 p.m. – 4:00 p.m. – Whip Practice in the Courtyard

4:30 p.m. – 5:30 p.m. – Fireplay: Turning Up the Heat

6:00 p.m. – 7:00 p.m. – Special Event: Littles Picnic

7:00 p.m. – 8:00 p.m. – Special Event: Rainbow Dinner

10:00 p.m.—11:00 p.m. – Special Event: Fetish Workers Meet and Greet

Pool

10:00 p.m.—1:00 a.m. – Special Event: Pool Party

Restaurant

3:00 p.m. – 4:00 p.m. – Special Event: Lip Service and Dirty Words. BDSM and Kink Writers Circl

8:30 p.m. – 9:30 p.m. – Volunteer Ice Cream Social

10:00 p.m.—11:00 p.m. – Special Event: Kinky Speed Dating

12:00 a.m. – 1:00 a.m. – Special Event: Go the Fuck to Sleep/ Midnight Snack

Saturday, July 6

Salon A

9:00 a.m. – 10:00 a.m. – Compression: The Art of the Squeeze

10:30 a.m. – 12:00 p.m. – Mean-eedles

1:00 p.m. – 2:00 p.m. – Genital Play or "How to Play with the Naughty Bits"

2:30 p.m. – 4:00 p.m. – Electric Staple Gun Play

4:30 p.m. – 5:30 p.m. – The Alpha Submissive: How to Yield Your Strength

8:00 p.m. – 9:00 p.m. – Dungeon Opens for Play

Salon B

9:00 a.m. – 10:00 a.m. – Service: What is it and Why do People Crave it?

10:30 a.m. – 12:00 p.m. – Advanced Whip Techniques for Dungeon Play

1:00 p.m. – 2:00 p.m. – Breathplay 201: AKA Don't Tell Jay Wiseman

2:30 p.m. – 4:00 p.m. – Playing When Health is a Hard Limit

4:30 p.m. – 5:30 p.m. – Successful Sex in the Age of SESTA, FOSTA

8:00 p.m. – 9:00 p.m. – Dungeon opens for play.

Salon C

9:00 a.m. – 10:00 a.m. – Rough Body Play and Wrestling

10:30 a.m. – 12:00 p.m. – Playing with Gravity: Partial Suspensions for Fun and Torture

1:00 p.m. – 2:00 p.m. – Invisible Bruises: Emotional First Aid

2:30 p.m. – 4:00 p.m. – Simple Physics for Advanced Rope

4:30 p.m. – 5:30 p.m. – Mermaid Ties

8:00 p.m. – 9:00 p.m. – Dungeon opens for play.

Salon D

9:00 a.m. – 10:00 a.m. – Conductive Rope

10:30 a.m. – 12:00 p.m. – Intro to Rope Bondage

1:00 p.m. – 2:00 p.m. – Foot Torture

2:30 p.m. – 4:00 p.m. – Advanced Flogging

4:30 p.m. – 5:30 p.m. – Real Service

8:00 p.m. – 9:00 p.m. – Dungeon open for play.

Salon E

9:00 a.m. – 10:00 a.m. – Hypnosis and Bondage

10:30 a.m. – 12:00 p.m. – Drugs, Potions, and Knockout Powders, Oh My

1:00 p.m. – 2:00 p.m. – Multilevel Mind Games

2:30 p.m. – 4:00 p.m. – Memory Play and Amnesia

4:30 p.m. – 5:30 p.m. – Hypnosis for Fear Play

8:00 p.m. – 9:00 p.m. – Special Event: Oral Recitation of Great Literature and Pornography

10:00 p.m. – 11:00 p.m. – Special Event: Hypno Lounge

Boardroom A

9:00 a.m. – 10:00 a.m. – Creative Sadism Taught by a Masochist

10:30 a.m. – 12:00 p.m. – Relationship Contracts

1:00 p.m. – 2:00 p.m. – Protocols 101

2:30 p.m. – 4:00 p.m. – Bosom Buddies: Tit Torture for Beginners

4:30 p.m. – 5:30 p.m. – Rollercoaster of Play: The Psychology of Subspace and Subdrop

Boardroom B

9:00 a.m. – 10:00 a.m. - Transformation

10:30 a.m. – 12:00 p.m. – Special Event: Puppy Mosh

1:00 p.m. – 2:00 p.m. – 1950s Living in Real Life

2:30 p.m. – 4:00 p.m. – Special Event: Light Daycare

4:30 p.m. – 5:30 p.m. – Animal Roleplay

Courtyard

10:30 a.m. – 12:00 p.m. – Deep Cleaning Your Filthy Whore with a Pressure Washer

1:00 p.m. – 2:00 p.m. – Sensual Fireplay

4:30 p.m. – 5:30 p.m. – Advanced Fireplay

8:00 p.m. – 9:00 p.m. – Special Event: POC Meet and Greet

9:00 p.m. – 10:00 p.m. – Special Event: M/s Meet and Greet

10:00 p.m. – 11:00 p.m. – Special Event: TNG Meet and Greet

Pool

2:30 p.m. – 4:00 p.m. – Water Bondage

Restaurant

9:00 p.m. – 11:00 p.m. – Special Event: Board Game Social

Sunday, July 7

Salon A

10:30 a.m. – 11:30 a.m. – Past is Prologue: Leather Histories for Modern Kink Communities

1:00 p.m. – 2:00 p.m. – Sexual Assault and Sexual Violence: Let's Talk About Consent

2:30 p.m. – 4:00 p.m. – Wielding Steel: An Advanced Knifeplay Experience

4:30 p.m. – 5:30 p.m. – Forced Orgasms and Orgasm Control

8:00 p.m. – 9:00 p.m. – Dungeon opens for play.

Salon B

10:30 a.m. – 11:30 a.m. – The Arse Class

1:00 p.m. – 2:00 p.m. – Cuckolding for Couples

2:30 p.m. – 4:00 p.m. – Cathartic Flogging

4:30 p.m. – 5:30 p.m. – Two Decades Plus of the Black Male Submissive Experience

8:00 p.m. – 9:00 p.m. – Dungeon Opens for Play

Salon C

10:30 a.m. – 11:30 a.m. – Increasing Your Accuracy

1:00 p.m. – 2:00 p.m. – Power Exchange and Communication Through Ballroom Dance-

2:30 p.m. – 4:00 p.m. – Introduction to Self Suspension

4:30 p.m. – 5:30 p.m. – Fear of Asking in Submissives

8:00 p.m. – 9:00 p.m. – Dungeon open for play.

Salon D

10:30 a.m. – 11:30 a.m. – Violet Wand 101

1:00 p.m. – 2:00 p.m. – Playing Without a Toybag: Punching, Slapping, Kicking

2:30 p.m. – 4:00 p.m. – Pallet Wrap Suspension

4:30 p.m. – 5:30 p.m. – Violet Wands 201/301

8:00 p.m. – 9:00 p.m. – Dungeon open for play.

Salon E

10:30 a.m. – 11:30 a.m. – Getting What You Want Without Going to Jail

1:00 p.m. – 2:00 p.m. – Sex Toys for All Kinds of Boys

2:30 p.m. – 4:00 p.m. – Put Heaven at Your Feet

4:30 p.m. – 5:30 p.m. – Hypnosis for Dominance and Submission

8:00 p.m. – 9:00 p.m. – Dungeon open for play

Boardroom A

10:30 a.m. – 11:30 a.m. – Saying Yes to Saying No

1:00 p.m. – 2:00 p.m. – Bootblacking 101

Boardroom B

10:30 a.m. – 11:30 a.m. - Ballbusting

Lounge

10:30 a.m. – 11:30 a.m. – Tea Service Class

11:45 a.m. – 2:00 p.m. – Special Event: TES Fest Kinky Tea

Well, if that isn't enough for a long weekend of sexual fun then nothing is! Terms you do not know can be looked up online at sexdictionary.com. If you do not want to wait for a festival, a fetishcon, or local underground workshops, then you can go online to FetLife.com. They have a group for all persuasions. In fact, they have hundreds, covering every iteration of play.

Earlier in this chapter I revealed a number of methods of figuring out your kink of choice. The next chapter further develops these self-awareness exercises and then some. You can never have too much kink!

CHAPTER 7

Discovering What You Want To Do That Perhaps You Did Not Know That You Want to Do and When to and Not to Do It

This book is full of ways in which a person or one's spouse, can discover that which they might want to try out in actuality, that is to say real life. Imaginative Relaxation is a safe way, beyond fantasy, where someone can get a sense of what they might want to effect in everyday life. Now whereas each of the specific techniques described later are designed to explore and manifest a particular sexual preference they can easily be adapted to the task of finding out which kink is your kink. Nonetheless you can get started figuring that out with the ideas I outline below.

So a great way to develop an inkling of how you might want to open up sexually is to read the erotic literature that is readily available. Nancy Friday, for example, has a number of books containing actual letters from women describing their sexual fantasies and/ or things they have actually done. Over the years there's been some change in the themes that dominate her volumes but nonetheless her books are full of ideas and suggestions that the reader might try out. These ideas run the full gamut from kink to fetish to fantasy play to swinging and everything in between. Thoughts, fantasies and realities involving sadomasochism, dominance and submission, and bondage also abound. By reading books like these the reader can get a clear sense of what they find boring versus what they find titillating. One needs to pay attention to what you know to be first vestiges of sexual interest and arousal inside of you. What is it that makes you as a man begin to get an erection? What is it that makes you as a woman begin to get aroused by lubricating? What is it that makes your penis or clitoris continued to swell?

Other erotic literature will serve a similar purpose. For example, there is over a decade of annual anthologies of the best American short story erotica edited by sex positive feminist pioneer Susie Bright. Readers can putter around choosing from the widest range of stories with titles such as "Mergers and Acquisitions," "My Professor," and "The Babysitter" (be careful about assumptions-it is the of age female babysitter who winds up seducing the mom!). Again, see what gives you that telltale sexual tingle, see what gets you hot and bothered, see what gets you turned on, notice what gets you horny. I generally don't recommend to people pornographic letter magazines like those which Penthouse publishes. These too often seem formulaic, contrived, and written by the same person.

Another way to explore that which you may want to try is to visit an upscale adult video store. It used to be that these were rather seedy places populated by creepy leering men. Without a doubt those still exist (and some like that atmosphere!), however, a new type of video store has cropped up, one which is women friendly. These often advertise themselves as welcoming women and couples and provide psychological and even physical safeguards to stop anyone from being bothered. Typically there is at least one woman behind the counter welcoming their gender. When in doubt it is always a good idea for the male half of the couple to visit the venue first to engage in reconnaissance regarding its acceptability. A good practical guideline is that when couples visit these video stores it should be the woman who wanders and selects the films. Sure, a man can pick what appeals to him, but it is less likely to interest the woman compared to when things happen the other way around. Generally, the road to a new erotic and kinky life runs through the female half of the partnership. Women tend to be the decision-makers as to what happens and what does not happen erotically. Of course, men should feel confident enough to hint, allude, suggest, and figure out new ideas, but it will be the woman in most cases who decides what gets actualized and to what extent.

Probably the most surefire way of figuring out what you might want to experiment with is to notice your masturbatory fantasies. The ones you start out with provide good information.

The ones you continue on with as you get excited provide great information. The one that you like to orgasm to provides the best information. The idea that makes you come and come hard is without a doubt the best clue as to what you may want to do. Of course, there are lots of fantasies that a person would not want to act out in everyday life. Elsewhere I take up the topic of how to distinguish between what should remain only a fantasy versus what might be enacted in reality. Of course there is a whole continuum in between these two extremes. For example, one of the most common female fantasies is to have anonymous sex. Of course this is too risky and too dangerous for almost everyone of us. Yet a couple could play out a hot variation of this fantasy by, for example, having a woman go into a classy lounge or bar alone and five minutes ahead of the male, only to have the male saunter in and pretend to be a stranger such that the two can play act a quick pickup. Safe but fun. It provides much of the upside of the orgastic fantasy with none of the downside. People need to understand that sexual freedom does not always involve enacting in full-blown form the ultimate orgastic fantasy. Iterations and attenuated variations most often suffice and can allow for the removal of objectionable, unsafe, or risky facets of the activity. And remember, above all, activity should be safe, sane and consensual.

Another great way to discover whether or not you wish to engage in a particular endeavor is to go to a public place where people are doing what you fantasize about. However, and this is an important caveat, the first time you do so you should visit strictly as "tourists." For example, most major cities have at least one public BDSM "dungeon." These are almost always clean, strictly monitored, and guideline- full venues. So long as you do not ever interrupt or talk to the participants during a "scene," you are free to wander around and view everything from spankings to foot worship to various forms of bondage to candle wax play etc. etc. etc. Until one visits such places it's impossible to imagine the multiple variations and iterations of that which turns people on. I remember being in New York City and going into a trendy but rather leather ridden bar and seeing a flyer advertising a future "stinky sock smelling night!" This was to be held at another bar that seemed to regularly feature activities that would appeal to foot fetish aficionados. But only in New York City could there possibly be enough people to make holding "stinky sock smelling night" a good business idea!

The same "tourist" approach can be taken to other venues as well, with other erotic themes. For example I always recommend to couples who have thoughts of swinging to first go to a swingers club and simply hang out and watch. This is never problematic so long as you don't not gawk and drool! Also, you may need to get naked or near naked or at least be wrapped in a towel to enter some areas. It's always a good idea to at least feign the impression that it is not your first time there and therefore not look like a "deer in headlights." In swingers clubs it's ubiquitously axiomatic that "no means no" such that a couple can wander around view activities ranging from seeing two couples slip into a private room and lock the door behind them to full-blown orgies. If somebody approaches you to hook up you can politely and nicely say something like "oh, thank you very much but we're good."

After the tourist phase, couples will have some idea as to whether they want to go further. Yet jumping into the deep end of the pool is never a good idea. Couples should play out what it might be like in fantasy in the privacy of their bedroom. Then, one member of the couple, usually the male, can volunteer to go on reconnaissance to a particular swingers club. If then they go to an actual venue they're always best advised to go slowly. Step by step. With swinging for example, couples can first allow themselves to be with each other only, yet watched. Later they may engage in same room sex separate from another couple or two. Still later, if they have a comfort level and want to go further, they could have sex with each other while being right next to another couple. And so forth and so on. This is referred to as "soft swing." The point is to go slowly and in a step-by-step fashion to avoid doing something that you regret. *Knowing when enough is enough and when to stop is at least as important as encouraging oneself to be open and free.* The balance between these two extremes is delicate so it should be monitored and both considerations kept in place at all times. When in doubt it's best not to do something new. A person can always go back at another time and engage in a particular activity. Yet there are some things that once you do them cannot be undone so it's best to inch up on them so that you can almost assuredly gauge your comfort level.

For now, suffice it to say that to discover that which you want to do that you did not know that you wanted to do is a matter of first exposing yourself to a plethora of possibilities and then gradually sampling that which appeals.

This brings up the question of how a couple, each of whom has identified their kink of choice, negotiates what they wind up doing *together*. The answer is that they take their personal preferences and see where there is overlap. If they get along as a couple then they probably going to get along as kinksters. An alternative is for each party to see where they can give to the other and be a "good sport" regarding some activity that doesn't exactly float their boat.

Great care should be exerted here however because some activities require a much greater buy in then others and hence should be examined very closely before the gas pedal is stepped on. For example, a woman dressing up as a schoolgirl or a guy donning a schoolboy outfit for their partner will be none the worse off if it all winds up somehow being an unpleasant experience. On the other hand the man or woman who accommodates their partner by participating in an orgy is likely to have to deal with some seriously negative emotions if the adventure turns out to be unpleasant. When deciding whether to be easy going or not about a sexual experience it is important to consider the amount of emotional buy in that is required.

Couples should also consider the consequences that might happen if a worst case scenario should occur. What could happen? Disease? Arrest? Political ambitions destroyed? Losing your dental practice? These possibilities need to be considered and deemed impossible, negligible or manageable. In the criminal community there is a saying . . . "if you can't do the time, don't do the crime." Something on that order applies here.

Here is a text exchange between a couple newly in love. They receive sex coaching from me. This is a very healthy example of how to negotiate the kink or wild in a relationship. He has been a diverse kinkster for years. She is quite conservative, but interested in opening up some, wanting to please him, and seeking to ensure he does not get bored with her sexually. Moreover, she is trying to get over feeling that fun sex is shameful. She also has her hands full in reconciling romantic sex with kink, role play, BDSM and the like. There are parts of the dialogue that are a bit difficult to follow. But hey, it is their messaging.

Beth: I've been thinking about where this whole notion of being kinky, etc comes from. You like to be kinky and "dirty" but either I'm not seeing all of you or what you think of as kinky and dirty really isn't as far down the kinky road as I thought it would be.

Jacques: Haha. Yea. I tuck it in a bit these days to tweak it for you. But that is how it should be.
But I do think u are wilder than u thought but it is hard for u to own it. Easier thou when u r aroused.
I also think it is FAR better for you to take initiative re that. I don't want to push.

Just so you don't feel caged or, not right word- haha, bet you'd find that kinky! Just so you don't feel restrained and bored after awhile.

I think worry keeps u from letting go some?
Worry that u won't do enough or be good enough.
But that is what is great about a bit of new kink. You feel brave and sexy. It is erotic to let go some.
I think too u worry about me getting bored so u don't want to try at all?

Beth: No. It's more the whole conservative moral thing that I had no idea how much was there in me—how strong the messages were/are. I've been really surprised about it.
But then, what I believe has never been challenged before. Or—I've just been surrounded by like thinkers.

Jacques: Oh I see
When we are together I will tell you about an idea I have that will feel ok n safe for you but will help u feel real sexy and hot.

Beth: I'm wondering if we both just let happen happen and not have to call it kinky or dirty—how that would be. What if we just let what our bodies want guide us. Just wondering. I wonder if there's sometimes an investment in some act being called kinky or sexy. What if it just is what our bodies want to do. What if sex is fulfilling or beautiful or sensuous or . . .
just wondering

Jacques: Yea, for u. I'm best off not being impulsive. It could be too much or the wrong kink
I think u should mainly lead n explore new stuff

Beth: What I'm saying is—philosophical.

What if "kink" and etc is really nothing but a reaction to breaking free of the limits, shame and restraints of religion. What if it's about enjoying what our bodies want to do.

Sometimes a movement has to swing totally the other way in order to break free. What if it's somewhere in the middle.

Jacques: Well put. Very. I couldn't have said it better!

Beth: So maybe you are a part of the swinging to the extreme movement in order for the generation after you to enjoy the healthy middle.

Jacques: But what u say is normal and healthy!!!! I on the other hand like to think kink cause then I get to break a taboo

Beth: Exactly!! You're on a mission. You're taking it to the far left in order to allow others to find their free place

Jacques: Not for psych folks but for other "kinksters" I am actually quite moderate.

In most ways.

Beth: Just throwing this out there-what if I'm in your life to not only help me break free but to allow yourself to not have to break the taboo but just be yourself—whatever that might be. Just be you and let go of the mission—at least in your private life.

Maybe you'll bring me from there right to the middle and I'll help you come down from the left and relaxed in the middle with me

Jacques: U have already done that for me. That's y I am cool not doing all the stuff I did before.

That being said I find it hot to help a person let go, however they define it! If u wore a burka I would want u to flash men ur eyes!!!!!

Beth: So I'm not just wondering all that. You have actually kind of been on a personal mission that you wanted/needed to be a part of privately for a good portion of your sex life?

F/U to the Catholic Church and your youth?

Jacques: Yes
Now I feel free to take stuff I like or leave it.

Beth: So can I ask, if you were to let go of the FU part, what would be you?

Jacques: Before ur last text . . .
I do not have obsessions or compulsions.

Beth: I'm thinking that leading a former nun down the free sex path just might be your final FU to religion, etc.

Jacques: I don't care about them. I just use the taboo to turbo-charge sex.
N to amuse myself n fuck with them. Ie. excommunication.
Last 2 were written prior to ur last text
Haha! Yes!

Beth: Yeah. I thought so.

Short story title. "Corrupting the Nun"
"The Decon and Debausherie"

That's what you're inviting me to do is it not- let go of the past and be in the moment and just experience you and me and us?

Jacques: Need what?

Beth: The joy of breaking taboos

So the "you without the joy . . . " It would be more extreme? The real you is more extreme.

Jacques: I was close to doing that.
But with you I found love, my top priority. So I happily adjust and feel content.

Beth: Interesting.

Same if spirituality was solely my goal. I wouldn't have u or fun Sex. I would meditate 6 hours a day as some do

Jacques: I get what you're saying. I'm seeking the way that says sexuality is not separate from good and fun sex. A whole person is fully into all parts of life—sex being a part of all of it.

Beth: Hey! U should go to sleep, eh?

Jacques: Yeah. I'm finally getting sleepy.

Night babe

Beth: I agree w ur last statement. We r on the same page.
Nite babe

By now you hopefully have some notion of what you wish to do and how that will mesh with your partners ideas about sex play. In the next chapter let's explore some ways to rid oneself of unwanted inhibitions and needless guilt.

CHAPTER 8

Deconstructing Unwanted Guilt, Shame and Inhibitions: Suggestions For Remodeling Your Conscience

"Dedicated to the countless men and women who have fought the lonely battle against guilt for doing sex acts that are neither harmful to themselves or others"

Albert Ellis, *Sex Without Guilt*

In writing that dedication to his 1958 landmark book Albert Ellis stepped up as one of the earliest mental health practitioners to sound a rallying cry for the active removal of unneeded sexual restraint. While most often thought of as one of the founding fathers of cognitive behavior therapy, his classic book identifies him as part of the triumvirate, with Kinsey and Hefner, that kick started the sexual revolution.

Albert Ellis saved my sexual life. To this day this remains my idea as to how best be "saved!" As a utterly inhibited and guilt ridden sixteen-year-old Catholic boy with an interest in psychology I somehow stumbled across this book. Without the aid of Imaginative Relaxation and being horridly unsuggestible to boot, my motivation, need, and determination enabled me nonetheless to kneed the healing messages into my sexual soul.

Imaginative Relaxation, however, does make this task much smoother, easier, and more doable. It is the tool that allows that which a person's conscious-mind-best-self deems needed to become operational at a subconscious and visceral level.

Many rather intimidating tomes have been written about the origins and vicissitudes of guilt and inhibitions. All are unuseful and even iatrogenic though because an in-depth knowledge of a problematic attitude will only afford us opportunity to eloquently create more of the same. In a healing, solution-focused life attention needs to paid primarily to deconstructing and removing inhibitions. Simply put, what we need to know about guilt and inhibitions is that they are often generated by well-intentioned parents, clergy, medical professionals, and the like who use their power, authority, and influence to encourage individuals to feel badly about harmless erotic desires. Frequently young and/or vulnerable, these messages are often received while the person is in a very impressionable and even in an Imaginative Relaxation-like state. Childhood and church have often combined to create corrosive constraints. Enter Imaginative Relaxation—the ultimate process to allow for a demolition of these limitations, and then a construction of a desired erotic self.

Shame is similar to guilt in often unnecessarily limiting orgastic pleasure. While guilt involves a persons internalized conscience berating oneself for actions performed or wishes entertained, shame is the feeling that arises as one considers the real or imagined judgements of others vis-à-vis these same desires or behaviors. Shame also often needlessly limits or blocks full sexual pleasure.

Guilt and shame are not always undesirable experiences however. Guilt and shame, when needed but absent, allow perpetrators to take advantage of drunk women and men, adulating alter boys and girls, and idealizing graduate students as well as many others. Shame and guilt should only be obliterated when then a person can have safe, sane, and consensual sex fun. Importantly, guilt and shame also can be invaluable in allowing one to be true to thought out, examined, and desired values endorsed by an adult's conscious-mind-best-self. Moreover, it can serve one in helping preclude involvement in wild and wooly erotic situations that a person is not emotionally ready to handle at present or perhaps ever. For example someone who is characteristically insecure, jealous, and possessive is best off eschewing the temptation to watch their spouse being pleasured by another. When self-awareness and good judgement fail, guilt and shame can be a fine friend!

Apart from these cautionary points though it is now time to proclaim . . . "LET THE GAMES BEGIN!"

But just how you ask? Well, the very first step is to shed unneeded and unwanted shame and guilt baggage. Enter the very powerful tool of Imaginative Relaxation in service of redeciding what values you wish to allow to control your erotic adventures. At last you control this psychic event, not the bishop when you were eight, the teacher when you were twelve, the parent when you were fourteen, or the gynecologist when you were eighteen.

Here then is the protocol to follow to effect changes that will obviate burdensome guilt and shame.

- First, as always, do a Imaginative Relaxation induction (Chapter 4).
- Second, likewise, as always, adopt an openness to suggestion (Chapter 5).
- Third, develop metaphors for destroying old and delimiting sexual dictates.

The first two procedures you already know how to perform. Below find script examples of how to effect the third step.

"I can allow myself to experience in front of me a fire into which I throw the contents of my unwanted inhibitions. They can appear in contract form and be torn apart by me prior to tossing the bits into the flames."

"I can experience myself holding a contract that contains sexual prohibitions that I no longer find relevant or useful. I dig a ditch in a field, and, after ripping up the contract I bury it there. I then erect a small marker which records the approximate dates the prohibitions were put on me along with todays date. Above that I write or sculpt, 'Rest In Peace'. I can then go and write up a new contract that nullifies the first contract and sets forth the sexual principles I now wish to live by."

"I can go back in time until I am once again with the individual who is giving me messages that are guilt inducing regarding sex. I shake my head NO and tell him or her that they are misguided and they themselves have problems and hang-ups. I then tell them I am not going to follow their advise"

Suggestions like these deconstruct and thereby destroy old and unhelpful dictates that inhibit a healthy sexuality. Therefore they serve as ideal preludes to suggestions for a free and unencumbered sexual self. These come aplenty in the chapters that follow.

CHAPTER 9

Imaginative Relaxation (IR) Dreaming: Giving Yourself a "Wet" Dream

The research on Imaginative Relaxation and its effects on dreams is crystal clear. Not only can it be done, it can be done reliably.

This bodes well for anyone wanting to expand and enhance their sexuality in surprising ways. For example, you do not need to know what kind of erotic adventure is desired consciously, your subconscious will inform you! Moreover, lusty wishes, some already known, can be played out and experimented with in the safety of sleep. And Imaginative Relaxation dreams can be as vivid and real as a virtual reality experience and more—all senses firing at full tilt.

Advantageously, a person doesn't even need a partner! However, should one be sleeping next to an amenable person an erotic dream can progress into a frothy fantasy-laden middle-of-the-night trial run. This movement from mental activity, however vivid, into action, is great progress toward perhaps enacting these fantasies in real life. Of course, not everything that is enjoyable in its utter debauchery in a dream state should be enacted in everyday life. Yet, the freedom of the dream state allows for an opportunity to try out innumerable scenarios and test their acceptability for use in everyday life. No partner present? Then this is masturbatory middle ground. But of course most of us would prefer a willing-partner-to-play-along-in-fantasy middle ground that would be acceptable instead of enactment in "real life."

To implement Imaginative Relaxation dreaming one can follow this protocol:

1. Prior to going to sleep, begin using Imaginative Relaxation or use during a daytime reverie with IR to induce a kinky wet daydream. And yes, women can not only have wet night dreams but they can also have wet daydreams. Moreover, these can happen without them even touching themselves.

2. So here is what you do . . .

3. Induction of self

4. Adopt a responsiveness to suggestion mind set

5. Give oneself suggestions for fun, safe, exciting and new erotic adventures to be played out in one's dreams

6. Use multiple specific alternatives—the subconscious thrives on choice!

7. Give oneself permission to respond by masturbating in or outside the sleep state or hint and approach one's partner if you have someone sleeping with you

8. In the morning or during middle of the night begin sharing the elements of the dream or dreams to gauge your partners response to the content/fantasy. If they are receptive or turned on then share more and more details. These are steps toward mutually agreed upon real life enactment.

Examples of how this might sound might include:

1. "I can have this hot erotic dream as the first or third or fourth dream of the night—or all three. Each can be different from or a continuation of the first."

2. "I can dream it in color or black & white."

3. "My erotic adventure can be like a snapshot photo, or a short video clip, or a short film or even a feature length film."

4. "It can be vivid, using all my senses—sight, sound, smell, taste, and touch."

5. "The dream can be utterly lifelike or can be like a virtual reality experience where I have some control over the direction it takes."

6. "I can remember the dream in the morning, that would be nice, or not, but either way it can have a positive influence

on my sexuality through the day and beyond. Everyone has had the experience of having a sex dream and having the sexual feeling carry you through the day. Now I am going to do that "

Obviously no ending of IR is needed since one is falling off to sleep or into a daydream revery.

It would be useful to journal experiences in Imaginative Relaxation dreaming for present or future pleasure and insight.

Overall, my advice is:

> "Follow your dreams, and follow your daydreams . . .
> they contain much information that you don't know
> that you know . . ."
>
> Dr. John H. Edgette

Here's hoping you and the sandman have a raucously hot time together!

CHAPTER 10

Extending and Developing your Kink of Choice: Writing Erotica

O nce changes are underway in a couple's or individual's sex life, the issue becomes one of how to extend these erotic developments. It's easy for old habits to set in once again and thereby bring with them a new bout of sexual doldrums. Individuals and couples can ensure the continuity of the desired erotic changes in their life by participating in a number of ongoing endeavors. These of course could involve reading additional erotic literature or by participating in erotic photoshoots, erotic videography, enjoying erotic artwork, watching erotic or sex-positive pornography, or any number of activities that enhance sexuality.

The writer of the short story I've reprinted below (with her permission of course) chose the avenue of writing erotic literature in order to keep her "juices" flowing. Hate it or love it, this is one woman's attempt to re-inculcate herself with lustful longings. She had already begun to participate in an increasing amount of exhibitionism and public sex, activities that thrilled her and were encouraged by her partner.

Note that at the start she takes the artistic liberty of using a number of different titles for this short story. When I asked her about this, she very creatively and matter-of-factly wondered aloud as to why stories should be limited to only one title! So here follows one woman's attempt at writing erotic short fiction:

***

Juliette's Improper Moment
Juliette's Moist Moment
Moist
Juliette's Skirt
Juliette After Golf
Juliette Alive, Coming & Going
When Charlotte Got Wet
Becoming Improper Again
The Importance of Being Improper Again
What Was to Inevitably Come
That Which Was to Inevitably Come

She wasn't used to this kind of attention. Not that she was frumpy, dumpy, or anything. But she looked *momish*, honestly.

No one would ever, she thought, use the words "hot" or "MILF" when regarding her. Not that she courted it, quite the contrary, she looked respectable, fit in with the other Catholic moms and, in short, had propertized herself.

So why was he staring at her . . . legs? Her golf skirt was knee length, plain, and proper, this she knew. But she also noticed herself now regretting its length, and subtly hiding the non-golf stains. With amusement and just a tinge of guilt she observed it riding up slowly. That itself wasn't out of the ordinary, but what was was her inability to take a moment to tug it down. For the first time in decades Juliette began to think "immodest" thoughts. Dirty thoughts. Bad girl thoughts. She began to feel warm down below. Moist. Alive.

He was nothing special. Nondescript, yet somehow more sharply dressed than the other country club men. No wrinkles, yet not affected. No Rolex, but a classy watch. And watch he did!

The terrace at the county club was two-tiered. A half step lower down, he was to be treated to whatever girl view he was allowed. Juliette began to feel generous.

His gaze at her legs was neither creepy nor rude. In the afternoon lull, it was obvious only to her.

Words like "no tablecloths," and "no one will know," came to her as if she were being possessed. "If this is the work of the Devil, I'll gladly go to hell in a hand basket," she thought, and then surprisingly only regretted the old fashioned nature of the statement.

Suppose he knows Frank? Suppose he is going to be one of my kids' coaches? Her secret Satan simply said, "Do it" then "just play dumb." She re-crossed her legs. The skirt ran up. No tug. She knew he could see inside her upper thighs. Funny, she thought, how legs crossed properly can show more than uncrossed and together.

Juliette thought back to college when her new boyfriend, Kyle (thank . . . er . . . God they were together for five fabulous lust-ridden years), had gotten her worked up in a then alarming way. Close to that typical fast, first-time fuck cum he stopped abruptly and would only continue if she spread her legs far and apart and lifted them high up. "Slutty wide" is what he ordered—and she did it. Then straight up in the air, toes pointed. Then holding her legs open with her own hands! She was used to how the boys liked her to moan, but this was way beyond that! Why, when he even stopped again and again until she would say louder and louder "Fuck my cunt hard" over and over. That was perhaps the first time she had "played dumb," knowing all the while that he wanted his friends in the hall to hear. Months later, he "made" (she promoted the idea) her repeat this performance in front of his roommate and then had her jerk him off while he watched and boasted of her technique. When she played with herself for them she came hard and then cried. Not a bad cry, not a good cry, a full cry of liberation. Juliette, improper and alive.

She didn't like her next thought. She and Frank hadn't mentioned the threesome they had when they were first engaged for decades. She put it out of her head with the "erase the blackboard" technique her Christian counselor had taught her.

Her lunch friends had left—only one raised eyebrow at the Mojito she decided to order, briefly justifying it with a gush of "Time Magazine, alone time before helping the kids with their homework."

Juliette had forgotten how good she was at playing dumb. She remembered Kyle making her change nonchalantly in front of the very cracked, first floor hotel blinds. Then later as the hotel bar emptied out onto the 2:00 a.m. street . . . doggie style, blinds more cracked, slurpy blow job, sit on him, couch close to window, ordered to spread her own ass cheeks, window open, sounds heard, let them hear. You come baby, do it for me, they like it, no one knows you here, sit on him backwards now, legs outside his, lean back, open up, then KY, up her ass, spreading her lips for them, made to touch herself to come. She remembered how she was never allowed to wear panties with him and how embarrassingly wet it always made her. She remembered all the husbands Kyle made her tease. He chose the stores carefully for their changing rooms. Curtains left quite cracked "by mistake." Dress. Lingerie. Bathing suits. Then she remembered the faces of the appreciative truckers on their car trips, "giving them a treat" he called it.

Juliette "absent-mindedly" opened her legs. Puffy. Swollen. Gushing. She didn't know how she knew that yellow was actually the most transparent color when wet, just secretly glad at her fortunate choice of panty that day. She slid down the seat, turning a page of the magazine propped in front of her face. She let her leg swing open, further, enough so she knew he could see how soaked she was. Her slide move also meant he could see the outer lip of her pussy. Though it was a proper choice at the time, she was glad her one piece outer banks swim suit had required her to shave and trim such that he could now see her own outer banks glisten.

It has been all too long since she had felt the mini lightning bolt go from her stomach to her pelvis and on to her puss.

She held her position. He held his gaze.

Moist
Wet
Wetter
Gush
Panty soak
Clit bulge
Lips spread themselves
Unctuous
Extreme unctuous

Juliette smiled a bad girl, Catholic smile at that one.

Juliette slid down a bit more but in a way that ensured her panty would get tighter then go up her cunt crack.

She wasn't sure if it was Kyle's voice or hers inside her head or a mixture, but the order was very clear "let him see your horny hole, let him see your horny fuck hole."

Ed was a good dad. Ed was a good provider. But Ed didn't provide for her pussy and Ed never called out "Who's your daddy" when fucking her. In fact, Ed never fucked. Ed had intercourse. Ed didn't lick her cunt, Ed performed cunnilingus. Ed didn't stick his finger up her butt, Ed always asked her to shower before sex so she was "cleany, clean."

Juliette pretended she had to scratch her upper thigh from a bug bite. Then she touched her clit briefly, just a flick was all she needed.

Juliette came.

Hard.

She cried a full quiet and discreet cry, and to her delight she felt no shame or guilt, nor any rush to exit. She briefly made eye contact with him, then was proud of herself as she smiled a bit, and nodded a bit, to acknowledge the tryst and give a private thanks.

Volvo keys in hand, she left, straight to the lawyer's office.

***

As you have just read, writing a work of fiction is just one way to nudge along pervy predilections. I have mentioned others at the start of this chapter. If you or your partner have trouble getting started with this or other developmental exercises, they can be done while in Imaginative Relaxation. Just go under, slowly open your eyes, and instruct your hand to write down your unconscious sexual wishes. It can be stream of consciousness.

By the way, this method can be used to discover your kinky self if you haven't already. Just let your subconscious surprise you!

CHAPTER 11

Bound to Happen:
The Future of *Your* BDSM

A ge progression or future progression is something you can experience in IR. It can allow one's subconscious mind to sample future potential realities. As such it becomes an invaluable tool for those interested in expanding their sexual repertoire. This, because it allows one to experience in a virtual reality kind of way what it would be like to actually do some of the things that you fantasize about. Whether it be BDSM, fantasy play, fetish, kink, or swinging, age progression enables a person to gain a sense of what it would be like to actually engage in wished for activities.

Future progression is an essential tool to help a person determine the viability of any sexual impulse. It provides you with a sneak preview of that which you think you want to do. This is essential because some fantasies can be acted out to immense satisfaction, whereas others should remain simply a fantasy because they would entail, once enacted, great psychological upheaval or stress for the individual or the couple. Both one's own mind and one's relationship should be prized and taken care of. Age progression is a method that allows a person to gain an important and essential inkling as to whether they wish to take that significant leap from having a mental wish to engaging in an actual activity.

While it is important for a person with their left brain or conscious mind to consider the outcome and ramifications of a sexual adventure that is a matter of logic and hence, it becomes really important for the person in IR to gain a sense as to whether their deeper or subconscious self can accept the escapade at hand. I've worked with many couples who've engaged in anything from spanking to swinging and come away tremendously closer and more fulfilled both as individuals and as a couple. I've also worked with individuals that engage in some sexual escapade only to afterward find themselves riddled with guilt or regret.

Age progression helps preclude problematic outcomes by giving people a safe psychic taste test of what they might want to try. As such, it becomes an essential way to figure out one's comfort level with some new notion for one's sex life. It is an essential way to protect oneself and one's relationship. The more radical the sexual adventure and the greater the "buy-in" for an individual or couple, the more important it becomes to assess the emotional and psychological viability of the activity.

From the contents of this book it is clear that I promote a full, liberal, and free sexuality. It should also be clear that I wish to ensure that in opening up no one does something that causes them to struggle emotionally. Age progression therefore allows a person to try something on for size and in so doing gain a sense as to whether they will genuinely enjoy it or whether there will be psychological fallout.

While most people unnecessarily inhibit themselves, a portion of people are too impulsive. This is where self-awareness comes into play. A person should know whether they are historically prone to regretting passing up opportunities or whether they are prone to regretting acting impulsively.

In age progression, a person fast forwards into the future and thereby allows their subconscious mind to imagine what it would be like to have a certain bit of fun. It is one thing to think about how you'll feel after feeling a new impulse and quite another to use your subconscious to "feel" how it will go. After this experiment some will masturbate furiously, while others will say, "Oh no, not for me." That is how it should be.

To effect age progression one needs to first use one or more induction strategies to go down into an IR state. Afterwards, one needs to activate the "I wish for" mind set described in Chapter 3. Then, added to these two essential prerequisites, a person needs to devise some tool for psychically moving into the future. This could be a time machine, a paper calendar that flips forward, going forward in a smart phone or iPad calendar, or imagining flying forward faster than the speed of light and arriving in the future.

Then give yourself suggestions for vividly, using all your senses, experiencing the first vestiges or beginnings of the sexual wish. That is for starters. Future IR sessions can sequentially have you experiencing more and more additional aspects of the wished for fantasy. After each session emotional reactions, as well as pleasure, should be noted. It is vital that the pleasure outstrips the discomfort, and that any negative emotional reaction is resolvable. It is also important to note any negative emotion that is experienced if it is a byproduct of unwanted values that were internalized unnecessarily in one's youth. These should then be challenged.

There are reasons for reticence that should be respected, but there are also more reasons for reticence that should be resolved and revolutionized. For both the individual and the partner. Remember, activities should be consensual and involve safe sex practices. On top of this, activities should conform to chosen values of the individual and/or couple. This, of course, is in distinction to values that were inserted into a person unwillingly via family or religious propaganda. These later dictates should be ritualistically overthrown via conscious intent and subconscious IR methods.

Some ways that future progression suggestions might sound being said or thought of are as follows. These are actual examples of what I said to a client in a session with her partner. The examples below relate to BDSM, but the content can be changed if one is interested in exploring fetish, Dom/sub, swinging, or other kinky pursuits.

"You experience yourself in a time machine moving forward in time to a year from now. You and your partner are together in this machine. You arrive in a public BDSM play space or "dungeon." You feel secure because you have your safe word, the word you can mention that will stop any activity. Your partner knows this word as well and it allows him to confidently pull out from his pocket a blindfold and put it on you. As people mingle you need to rely on your partner to lead you around and this begins to get you aroused."

"You see a monthly paper calendar in front of you and about twelve pages begin flipping off. You've moved forward one year in your life. You look up from the sight and sound of those calendar pages flying away to find yourself back in that public "dungeon." You're blindfolded once again. Now your partner goes further in having you sit on some type of wooden bench. He gently takes your hands and raises them and spreads them till they're stretched out at your side, fully extended at shoulder height. There is wood behind each arm and hand, and you feign surprise as each wrist is secured in place with a strap. Using your safe word is the furthest thing from your mind; so, too, are your legs spread open and your ankles are secured with a similar strap."

"You find yourself flying forward in time on a magic carpet. You whisk through cloud after cloud as you are transported to a future place. Down below you can see a road which represents a timeline and by observing this road you see that you've flown forward through one year. You decide to land and when you do you are pleased to see that you are once again in that "dungeon." Blindfolded, bound at your wrists and ankles, you know that a mere mention of your safe word would have your partner stop that which you are actually enjoying being done to you. Though you have mentioned this fantasy to him before, doing it is even more thrilling. As you hear people milling around, you feel him begin to undress you. Button by button your blouse is opened. Then, your skirt is unzipped and tugged down to your ankles. Now you know why you were "told" not to wear a bra or panties tonight. You feel as if you could orgasm without even being touched. Then you do."

These are three examples of how age progression can sequentially provide a sensitive indication as to whether or not a fantasy would be comfortable when being enacted. I have used a bondage theme coupled with an exhibitionistic theme to illustrate one example of some content that might be sampled once age progression has been realized. Again, any sexual predilection or preference could be substituted for this theme. The most important point to note is that no matter what the content, age progression or future progression can be used to enable a person over time to assess their comfort level with enacting a sexual adventure. The next chapter will give additional tips as to how a person can gain advanced knowledge regarding the advisability of turning thoughts into action.

PART THREE

YOUR BODY OF WORK

CHAPTER 12

Imaginative Relaxation for Breast Enlargement

There have been a number of published and unpublished research studies showing that Imaginative Relaxation breast augmentation is most achievable. In addition, there have been a great many case studies that have likewise shown the possibility of accomplishing this type of enhancement. Most commonly the result was that after a month of interpersonal (someone talking you through it) and self-Imaginative Relaxation practice shows a breast size increase of the half a cup or more.

The protocol is ludicrously simple and straightforward. In most instances, the IR leader suggests that the subject vividly experience psychologically, as if it's virtual reality, a warm blanket covering both breasts and staying warm. Subjects are asked to practice this a couple times a day for ten or fifteen minutes.

After putting yourself in an Imaginative Relaxation state the suggestions for intervention would sound something like this:

"I can, with all my senses, have the experience right now of a very nice warm blanket laying on my chest. It can be made out of any material I wish and amazingly it holds the warmth quite nicely and having optimal temperature for breast growth. An alternative that is perfectly and totally acceptable is for me to imagine that this blanket is an electric blanket and I can adjust the heat in an ongoing fashion, again perfect for breast enlargement. Over time and in time my breast size can increase in numerous ways. It might be the width of my breast, how they come forward and lift up, or how firm they are, or all three of these changes."

Or . . .

"I am comfortable with the overall size and shape of my breasts, however I feel as if they could be firmer. So that is the experience I can now have. It's beyond imagination, it is like a virtual reality experience. Gosh, I can feel it happening! Boobs firm, pert, standing upright and quite forward. Firm yet also pleasantly soft and supple. Any change that I desire can be actualized."

The reason this works is that blood flow is notoriously adjustable and controllable using Imaginative Relaxation. During minor or major surgery, during dental work, the suggestion can be made that blood only needs to come out of the wound or incision to the extent that is needed for cleansing and to reduce infection. That the amount of blood loss during procedures is possible has been chronicled numerous times.

Additionally, blood flow can be increased such that a lab technician drawing blood can accomplish this task more easily. Also, foot neuropathy can be alleviated by suggesting increased blood flow to the lower extremities. Venus insufficiency, usually to the lower legs, can be ameliorated. Reynolds disease can be remediated. Likewise, phantom limb pain (where an amputated part of the body that no longer exists but is sensed as if it does) can be precluded or eliminated by increasing the amount of blood that resides in the area near the amputation . Moreover, as has been documented in the next chapter, erections can be enhanced through IR by moving more blood to the penis.

There are other ways to increase blood flow to a woman's breasts other than the warm blanket method period she could, for example imagine water faucet or spigot sending an ever increasing amount of blood flow to the breasts.

There are other ways in which Imaginative Relaxation can be employed to accomplish the goal at hand. Probably the best thing to use is age regression. With this one is encouraged to go back in time to every day biological moments where breast size naturally increases. We often don't realize how breast size growth is often a part of normal biological hormonal rhythms. There are so many examples of this. Upon reaching puberty, a girl becoming a woman suddenly evidences an ever growing swelling of her breasts. And at some point around each month's menstrual period breasts grow larger. Likewise when a woman is a certain length of time into her pregnancy her breasts grow. The common expression for this is that she is visited by the "tit fairy."

Suggestions to capitalize on the naturally occurring breast augmentation that are part of physiological development for a woman might sound as follows . . .

"I can go back in time, time traveling as if I am in a time machine, or riding a train, plane, or automobile on the road back to breast bigger. I can stop at various roadside scenes and rest stops that crop up along the way. At each stop there is one example of a time when my boobs grew. I can see personal historical markers and witness personal historical places that enact what I have experienced as a part of bigger boob everyday life. Every adult woman, including myself, reached the age where she began to menstruate, or her body prepared to do such. At the first roadside stop I see a scene showing me in a t-shirt, my titties having swollen. Moving along I come to another station that every woman who has had children or knows someone who has had kids is familiar with. Witness my or her breasts get larger in anticipation of the breastfeeding that is to come. Wow!"

In any event, this is the kind of suggestion that can be experienced to accomplish the goal of bigger and better boobs. That the research results are consistent and quite impressive is inspiring. Moreover one cannot object to the lack of expense that this method entails compared to surgical augmentation.

Next we move on to the novel, experimental and interesting application of IR to penis enlargement!

CHAPTER 13

Penis Enlargement: When a Rock Hard 8 Isn't Enough

A number of years ago a man came to me for help with weight control. He wanted to lose about fifty pounds, and indeed he needed to. He wanted to work with me in particular because I had developed the powerful change technique of Imaginative Relaxation, which he had read about and his friends had raved about.

During the initial interview it became clear that changes in diet and exercise were in order. Of course. How could it be otherwise? We jointly decided (yes, these needed to be "joint" decisions as you will see) to use Imaginative Relaxation to take him time traveling back to when he was once at his goal weight, have him lock that in with suggestions for photographic memory, and then have him drag and drop it into a future time. This would give him hope, motivation, and a goal. It would serve as a magnet drawing him toward what he would experience as an inevitable future of thinness.

Okay, but by now you are thinking that this was supposed to be a chapter about penis enlargement right? Well hold tight, we are getting there.

Toward the end of the interview he hesitantly said . . . , "Well, Doc I have to tell you that I don't just want to lose weight, I want it to go to a particular place in my body." Eyebrows raised, I asked him what he had in mind. He answered excitedly "I want it to go right to my dick. I want it to grow and enlarge and expand."

It took me a moment to regain my composure! No practitioner had ever attempted such a thing before.

I wound up saying to him, "Well, Lionel, I will attempt that for you but I have to inform you that this will be an experimental procedure, so I can't promise any results." He then indicated that he understood.

After a couple of days I mustered up the audacity to ask him his vitals. This was not something I was used to doing! But at the start of the next session I gathered up my courage and asked him for his specs. Unflinchingly he said "the length is currently eight inches, the width is an inch and a half, and the height is three quarters of an inch." Somehow I managed not to flinch. It was one of those moments where, as a helper, you want to burst into a philosophical laughter but you know the client will think you are laughing at them, not at the wild and wonderful world of penile possibilities. But I was able to keep my professional poker face.

I then asked about the goal he wanted to attain. He said, "I would like to have ten total inches in length, another half an inch of width, and another quarter of an inch in height." Now, Lionel was from an ethnicity renowned for the large size of male members but this was a quest for a porn-star penis! I was developing penis envy. Big time.

In the second and third sessions, we did Imaginative Relaxation. I taught him how to do it so that he could reinforce our work at home. He was an eager and motivated student.

In terms of suggestions for weight loss I gave him imaginings in line with the ideas I mentioned above. And then I turned to working on the goal of penis enlargement. Suggestions were first given for him to visualize his body fat breaking up and traveling to his male meat (I use as many words for the body part as possible so as to be sure the subconscious gets the message. Variety makes this happen more easily). The ideas I presented to him, and wanted him to remember and review at home, went something like this:

"You can experience your body fat breaking up . . . almost like those TV commercials where detergent is put on a stain then placed in water. The solid of the stain breaks into little pieces and floats away. See and experience your body doing this *now*. And where do these pieces float to? They go one by one into miniature open train cars, the kind that transports coal. Perhaps

HO in *size*, maybe *larger*. They then ride from all directions on scale model train tracks directly to your dick. They are all express trains converging on your cock from different lines and limbs. Down the arms and up the legs, all on a mission to reach that one final destination. Once there, a crane takes the fat particles and deposits them at the base of that funnel shoot called a *schlong*. From there, the pieces and particles travel down that shoot and take up residence, from the tip on up, kind of like a corn silo. There they remain, making the penis so full it's stretchy material expands from tip to base as well as the sides, the top and the bottom."

Lionel really liked these images. That was in part because he was a model train enthusiast. I knew this from that first interview as well as from the fact that he played with trains with his kids. They had three large layouts in a very big basement. All trains actually had multiple train cars transporting coal. When they arrived at a riverside depot, a crane took the coal and swung it to the top of the shoot where it filled up waiting barges. So the image fit, and fit well.

I was not done crafting Lionel's personal imaginal change world. Next, I taught him how to give clues to his body such that he anticipated penile change. With anticipation comes expectation and expectation is the magnet that brings to fruition the hopes inherent in the law of attraction. That is, hope and expectation provide the opportunity for wishes to be actualized. So here is what I said . . .

"Every male has had the experience of having his cock enlarge and grow. Remember back to when you were a teenager and you got those first teenage erections. Often you would pop one randomly. Yet, you knew it would swell and become engorged for certain if you thought of girls. And month by month it grew, sometimes gradually and sometimes abruptly. You can remember all this vividly and with all your senses. And you can wish for it to happen just like that again and again now. You can go even further back in time and perhaps recall the times when you were a baby, and then a toddler and then then a boy . . . experiencing penis growth at various times. Times like when you played in the soapy bathtub and it felt all slippery and tingly. Or when you had one or both of your hands below the covers and felt the warm and fuzzy blanket on it. It felt so good and it could expand. Why should any of this stop there and then. It can happen again now. Your body already knows how to do this. Your penis can grow and enlarge and expand beyond its current size and beyond the current boundaries now, as it once did then. Your body knows a lot more than you think it knows."

Lionel returned for a follow up session six months later. He had been practicing creating the scenes in Imaginative Relaxation. He was thrilled that he had lost twenty-five pounds and he anticipated losing the rest of the weight he wanted in the months to follow. He then said that he was disappointed in the results of the penis enlargement work. I was about to remind him that it was experimental work and that I had given him no guarantee that we would be successful. But then I stopped myself, realizing that I was just assuming that no change had taken place. I asked him what results he did get. "Well, Doc, my dick only increased an inch to nine inches and not ten." It only went up a quarter of an inch in width and an eighth of an inch in height . . . I only achieved half of what I wanted." I kept my best poker face once again while thinking to myself, "You greedy son-of-a-bitch!"

I explained to Lionel once again that this was an utterly experimental procedure. I also suggested that it was possible that he got half the results because he was only about half way to his weight loss goal. He liked that idea.

To do this for yourself put yourself in an IR state. Then think these thoughts in the first person. So "you" becomes "I" etc. Alternately you can have a friend put you into IR and read a variation of what I said to Lionel without having to change tenses.

As for Lionel himself, I will know whether "the rich get richer" in another six months when we have or next followup session! Stay tuned!

Next, I devote an entire section of this book to that which Lionel and his partner might want to do with his newly found endowment. You might want to venture forth into that world, too. It is called swinging!

PART FOUR

COVET THY NEIGHBOR'S WIFE (OR HUSBAND)

CHAPTER 14

Avoiding "Rookie Errors" When Swinging (or Kinking)

Swinging isn't what it used to be, or what it was thought to once be. Not a "key swap" and for sure not the horridly sexist idea of "wife-swapping." This newly revitalized popular activity mainly has women running and managing the clubs. *Women run the fun from New York to L.A. to Jamaica to Mexico and beyond, as well as innumerable venues in between.*

How many people already swing? Investigative reporter Terry Gould estimates that there are over 3 million people in "the lifestyle" in North America. It is hard to imagine how many people engaging in this often clandestine act were never counted. It is even harder to imagine how many wish to play in this way but do not know how to get started or are intimidated.

What is known is that Joel Stein in Time magazine asks "Why should our last threesome have been in college"?

Oprah exclaims at the end of an interview with a swinging couple "Sounds like a lot of fun!"

Even way back on the July 3rd, 2011, Sunday New York Times Magazine cover author Mark Oppenheimer summarizes his interview with America's leading sex columnist Dan Savage with the article title "Infidelity Keeps Us Together: reconsidering what makes a healthy marriage."

On the cusp of the people who do swing are hundreds of thousands, perhaps millions, who are ready but don't know how to start, or who are less sure but fantasize and fantasize.

If you are one of these folks read on. You have found the right place. You are home. Let's start by talking about the six most common errors people make when starting out. With each we will discuss what it is you should do.

When a couple decides to try out the swinging scene, at whatever level, there are six things they should avoid in order to preclude a bad experience. As we will note later, awkward, even painful experiences can happen regardless, and need to be dealt with at the time, but that doesn't mean a couple should naively walk headlong into them. Avoiding common mistakes safeguards a relationship and helps ensure a smooth transition into swinging. These are common mistakes because many people make them. Noting them and the methods to avoid them are the result of

much psychological observation by the author and solution finding in response to the observations.

Oh yes! By the way, the six pieces of advise related to swinging can and should be modified by anyone new to Kink, Fetish,
BDSM, and Dom/sub play. Most of the points are relevant and
can be adapted to your play of choice.

Imaginative Relaxation can be utilized in ensuring that these
six mistakes are avoided and that six positive alternatives can be
dropped into the subconscious. This is a good way to prevent the
mistakes from taking place in the heat of the moment.

Going too quickly into swinging is probably the number one error
people make. Going slowly is the antidote. To ensure comfort
couples, no matter what their fantasies, should progress slowly
through the seven stages noted in the next chapter, Chapter 14.

Julie and Jim decided they wanted to try swinging. They went to
an established New York City swing club that advertised, "There
are no strangers here, just friends we haven't met yet." A bit
'60s/'70s of a slogan, no doubt, but they went nonetheless.

After waiting in line for a half an hour with other couples (this
club does not allow single males at all) they went in and used
fake names since this was perhaps the only club that does not
require ID or a last name. So "Jocko and Madison" made their
way into the bar area. Julie was nervous but wanted to play like a
good sport, much as she had once done in her teens and twenties
before these fifteen years of marriage and five years of fantasizing
with Jim about other partners.

So Julie took an Ativan and made sure it went down by doing four shots of Absolute vodka. They had actually forgotten to bring any liquor so one of the bouncers had obliged by going into an attic and returning with a bottle of Absolute for sale. Julie had wanted the red wine, but Jim wanted to loosen her up not knowing how drunk she would get. Throughout the night she showed no signs of inebriation. She was cogent, agile, and clear. Yet Julie would not remember the night.

By the time the club closed it was actually getting light out and they both stumbled out into the street feeling the weirdness one can only feel after partying all night in the dark only to have a door open to a 6:00 a.m. sunrise.

After six hours of sleep Julie confessed, over a decadent NYC brunch, her amnesia. Jim, surprised, nonetheless recounted the evening. The five guys she had after stripping into towels in a coed locker room, the orgy room, the sex swing, and him almost having sex without a condom . . .

It was a sad story. They fought for weeks. Julie, rather than taking responsibility for her indulgences somehow blamed Jim entirely for the debacle. Jim himself was defensive and not taking responsibility for attempting unprotected sex. "I only entered her a little bit before she kicked me off of her."

With my help, they again attempted (successfully!) swinging months later. Mission accomplished!

This example illustrates the kind of trouble that can be created by moving too fast and too deeply into the swinging world. It also illustrates a sub point. Don't drink or drug and swing or kink. Or at least don't drink much.

A second basic error is for the couple to go to a swing club for the first time together! It makes best sense for the man to go alone for the first time to scout things out. He should not engage in any activity, just scout out the scene. Then he should report back in detail about what to expect. This paves the way for comfort for the couple. Most clubs allow single men in on a Friday night and often on Saturday nights as well, (almost all are closed during the week). Being a spy for your wife helps ensure she knows what she is to expect.

Andrew volunteered to go check out the swing scene within the Philadelphia area. He visited "The Farm," "The Cottage," "TJ's Lasting Impressions," and "The Private Affair," all within hours of the city. His reconnaissance allowed them to pick a venue that suited them (all places differ in atmosphere, for example some are classy while others are purposefully somewhat raw, sleazy, and raunchy). They then went together and had a great time while obeying the cardinal rule to just watch and not participate the first time.

On the other hand, Johann visited Philadelphia's "Pleasure Garden Club" and gave a vivid description to his wife Marge. He described how it was upscale with a young hip urban crowd, good food, but few private rooms. He also cautioned her that when you walk in you first encounter the orgy play area, replete with a sex swing, and that it might prove a bit intense at first. Marge took this all in and they headed off one night. Upon entry, Marge took a gander at the matted, huge orgy area, replete with twosomes, threesomes, foursomes, and moresomes, and was like a deer in headlights, despite Johan's cautions. She remained that way all night, and could not play at any level because she was in a shock of sorts, although she had been to other swing clubs before. The point is, try to look like it is not your first rodeo.

It pays to have the male partner scout out the place thoroughly and have the spouse take the picture being painted very seriously. The same holds true for an experienced swinging male taking an inexperienced but interested male friend for the first time to a club, he needs to inform even the most sophisticated buddy what to expect. This, for no reason other than the fact that gawking, drooling, and otherwise being creepy is rude and will not only mean that you won't have sex that night but will also likely mean you will be shunned.

The third rookie error is being too forward. A couple, and certainly not a single male, should not approach another couple and propose retreating to a private or semi-private room. For a male, coupled or single, the way to fun with the couple in question is through a male-to-male connection, beginning with small talk. You should not talk to the female partner, other than a simple greeting, and certainly not for an extended time. The same holds true if a woman initiates contact with another couple, she should connect with small talk to the other woman and let it go from there. Have a cocktail together and chat. What is going to happen will happen.

Gary and Elaine were at a swing club for their third time. Gary was smitten with this one women, Alesia, and started a conversation with her, bodies very close. When he asked her to dance her husband Bill appeared, drinks in hand. He intervened and danced with her himself, drinks placed on the cocktail table. After two dances they grabbed their drinks and wandered off, leaving Gary and Elaine standing around looking silly.

On the other hand, Bob and Jim were a duo of single straight men at a club. Jim, once shy yet having been successfully mentored by Bob, started up a conversation at a cocktail table with Steve and Fionia. Bob wandered over after a while and joined in the conversation. They all discovered that they were once from the same area and had also all, except Jim, visited Hedonism 2. Drinks flowed as did the cigarettes and chat. Seemingly out of the blue Steve asked Bob if he and Jim wanted to go to a back private room with himself and Fionia. Consensus was quick and positive. On the way there Steve set limits. He stated that Fionia was only into oral that night. Being smart men, Jim and Bob were fine with that. Clothes flew quickly once the door was shut. Fionia took both members in her mouth while Steve watched. When Steve announced that Fionia liked to have guys come on her face Bob came immediately, responding to the lewd invitation. Jim actually talked Steve and then Fionia into screwing. They went at it for a half an hour while Bob and Steve watched. After Jim came, Steve reached into a bag and brought out Fionias' vibrators. She assertively said she was not in the mood to put on that show and so everyone decided the foray was over. All four kinksters dressed and hugged and went back to the bar area to see what else the night might bring.

The road to the female, for the male, runs through the other male. The road to the male or couple for the female runs through the other woman.

A fourth beginner mistake is to not watch over your partner. An extreme example of this is playing in separate rooms. This is the stage seven described in the next chapter. It is a very advanced stage and downright risky for the couple that is even at an intermediate level. If your partner is drinking even moderately or is using drugs being in the same room becomes even more important. Watching over your partner helps ensure that nothing happens that they or you don't consent to.

Janice and Justin were youngish and somewhat innocent looking, even though they had been to swingers clubs on many different occasions . In the group room(read orgy room) Justin was receiving oral sex from a very attractive young brunette, probably in her twenties.

"You have a beautiful dick," she exclaimed, and Justin came upon hearing the complement. At that point he glanced over at Janice who was receiving oral pleasure from an unattached male. She was in ecstatic rapture. The man went to mount her and Justin noticed he did not have a condom on.

"Wrap it up or giddyup," Justin said assertively. The fellow did put on a rubber and Janice enjoyed her frothy foray.

In most places and cases men put on condoms before fucking (sorry, Intercourse is only an Amish town in Pennsylvania,) but sometimes they stupidly try to opportunistically get away without one. In most places and cases women ensure that a rubber is used. However, when compromised by substances or unaware of what you are doing in a group room or some such, partners need to watch over one another. Women are more at risk since although it's rare that a soberish women allow unprotected sex, a vulnerable woman may be prey to a foolish man who takes advantage of the moment. Men who have unsafe sex with an unknowing partner should be punished by the sex gods with an eternal case of blue balls (Blue Ball is also a town in an Amish community in Pennsylvania!).

A fifth big mistake is to not communicate through the evening and night. While it is best for couples to decide beforehand how far to go on a given night, realistically, alterations in the game plan do happen. When that occurs it is essential that the couple discuss the situation. Usually it is one of the partners who has an notion regarding something that has not been discussed. Good communication obviates the feeling of being left behind, or worse yet, of betrayal.

Tom and Karen were hanging out in one of the hallways at "The Private Affair," between private theme rooms, with some doors open, some closed, and some with just a chain across accommodating corridor voyeurs. Karen leaned up against a wall for a moment and along came a bold women in high heals that flashed every time her foot hit the floor. It was as if she had on a high-heal version of the kid sneakers that flash every time a foot hits the ground. She slowly approached Karen, took her head, and moved in for a kiss. It lasted and lasted. No harm done, Karen looked to Tom for approval, and got it. An empty room was then entered by the two women, Tom, and an assortment of single men. Flashy shoe girl then commented with glee, "It's just the two of us girls in here to satisfy all these guys!"

Tom caught Karen's eye and nodded his approval. They were experienced in the swinging scene but hadn't gone this far yet. Lit shoe girl exclaimed, "I'll take care of this one first!"

She motioned to Tom, who happily obliged. Karen was herself busy taking care of some of the troops while shoe girl started her phallus fest with Tom.

Afterward Karen and Tom went home happy and sated, reminiscing with laughter all the way. For weeks they talked hot and dirty about it during sex. For weeks they whispered about it with giggles, laughter, and slaps on the butt, while their three breakfast table bound young kids knew not what to make of it. Nor would they ever.

Good communication is even more important the more novice the swingers are. Moreover, it also becomes essential when a couple at any level of swinging decides to expand limits. Lack of good communication is fuel for the fire of arguments, jealousy, and feelings of betrayal.

A sixth enemy of successful swinging is developing an emotional attachment to those you have sex play with. While this would seem natural in a sense, it is best avoided. To do otherwise puts you in the navagatable but more treacherous waters of polyamory. Now there is certainly nothing wrong with polyamory, but it is a different activity, a different flavor, and a different emotional-sexual experience. And one that is way more difficult to make work.

So if swinging and experiencing different partners is your desire, then you best take your cue from what is the tradition in much of the male gay community—for many gay males emotional connection, attachment, and intimacy is kept separate or dissociated from sexual adventure. It is this dichotomy that keeps affectionate and loving relationships together while providing spice to life. Furthermore, these trysts often provide the fodder for sexual heat between the loving couple. The main point of all this that what is difficult for straight couples is engaging in these encounters separately. It is not recommended.

Athi and Indi wanted to save money by contacting people online to swing, rather then going to clubs. They were successful in connecting with Reardon and Randi. They went out to dinner, had a great time, and went back to a hotel for fun. It was everything they expected and more! The couples got together frequently and switched partners. Soon Athi and Indi got together with Reardon and Randi for dinner before actually going to a public swing club. Athi and Indi invited along good friends who swing but did not engage in swinging with them. The six of them got along well, even playing "Spin the Viagra" at the pub!

Yet when they got to the club it wasn't long before Reardon and Randi insisted, in front of the guests that only Athi and Indi go to a private room alone with them. The guests were stunned by the rudeness of this, and the bolder male angrily yelled out, "You're ditching us!"

The night otherwise continued smoothly and pleasurably for all concerned, as far as they can all recall. Yet the next time Athi and Indi got together with their good friends for dinner before the club Randi and Reardon were missing. Athi related that Reardon and Randi had wanted an *exclusive* relationship between the four of them and it had weirded them out. The bolder male friend blurted out, "That's ridiculous! Playing with others is why you are swingers! Who asks for fidelity?" Laughter broke out around the table.

Other than cursory, courteous, and seductive conversations emotional attachments spell trouble for couples. That doesn't mean you are not polite when you see the couple or the single guy again, it just means you don't get attached. Emotional connections are way more dangerous to a couple than sexescapades.

In the next chapter we will look at the seven stages of swinging. In reading, keep in mind that the goal is not to get to level seven but to find the level for you that is comfortable yet exciting.

CHAPTER 15

How High Does The Swing Go? : The Seven Levels of Swinging

Kyle entered the largish hot tub at Hedo 2. Like any sensible single male at the resort he was polite and affable without trying too hard. It was 11:50 p.m. and the disco was actually emptying out and people were making their way to the nude side of the resort to enjoy the pool, enclosed private grotto, swim-up bar, and, of course, the popular hot tub. Kyle shared his story from the point of his sitting down in the immense hot tub:

"There was some space next to me, say a seat and a half, and I left it that way as I did not want to encroach on other couples. A couple came in and wound up 'sitting' next to me. She straddled him, facing away from him at first. Her hands were obviously busy below the bubbling water. She swam out to the middle of the hot tub dunked her head and swam back, straddling her guy, facing him this time. Her knee touched my hip, then her thigh was next to mine and her ankle was on my knee. I didn't move, I let her rub up against me, and happily. She turned toward me and asked where I was from. As I answered, 'St. Louis,' she nodded, closed her eyes, and most obviously impaled herself on his erection. Opening her eyes, she said, 'We're from Pittsburg.' Her legs were actually now moving in the utterly predictable yet utterly erotic sex tempo we all know. Yet she continued to converse with me, talking about jobs and family and the resort restaurants. Her tempo increased. Mid-sentence, Sue, as she had introduced herself mid-coitus, excused herself from the conversation 'He's about to come,' she said matter-of-factually, as if she were ordering a chablis. They finished, and as they did the utter heat of her leg picking up it's pace against mine was actually one of the most erotic experiences I have had in my lifetime. 'I'm Bill,' he offered, and the conversation continued as Sue went over to the swim-up bar for three purple passions."

As Kyle found out, and Sue and Bill enacted (not by error), swinging is not just one thing, it is a continuum of events.

This continuum can be considered to range from a 0 to 7 scale. Zero represents a man and a woman, neither of whom either have developed sexual fantasies or have no fantasies of swinging. It is just not on their radar.

Chad and Karen, for example, had a healthy sex life. When masturbating Chad would fantasize about blindfolding Karen.

Karen, when playing with herself, would think about being tied up and "forced" to have sex with Bill, over and over. When they had sex together they would, as most people do, typically evoke these fantasies to ever greater degrees, in order to orgasm, and moreover, "come good."

This is a good example of a 0 swinging couple. Sure, they have plenty of potential bondage fun ahead of them as they share their their fantasies, but swinging isn't their flavor of the month, or probably lifetime.

A number 1 level swinging couple would mean that one partner, either the man or women, has fantasies of swinging. Unlike Karen and Chad in the above example this couple will face the challenge of the one interested in swinging presenting it to the other. How to navigate this thorny thicket is the topic of another chapter.

Charlie and Mel loved to have sex. For reasons he did not understand he was turned on tremendously by the idea of her having sex with someone else. When they neared climax Charlie would tell her to pretend he was a particular ex-boyfriend, who he knew was good in bed. Inevitably, Mel would spread her legs further, talk "dirty," adopt lewder positions, and come. Charlie would come strongly and revel in the fantasy.

Charlie and Mel are a number 1 on the verge of becoming a number 2, where both partners show an interest with others. Once Mel begins talking about what she is thinking they move to a 2.

Mel did begin talking. One night, horny as she could be, she approached a distracted Charlie. "Want to hear about my grad school professor visiting me at my internship out of state? You know, he was there only to ensure my performance was up to expectations." Charlie's clothes littered the ground as he bolted for the bedroom. A bit later Charlie did in fact find out that in her internship Mel had exceeded expectations.

Stage 3 involves couples going to a swingers party or a swingers club open to the public. Here you can easily watch couples have sex, either with their partner or with others. In stage 3 it is best to be only a voyeur rather then do something you will regret. I have my curious clients promise that to themselves.

Sher and Tom made that therapeutic promise. They went to a club about an hour away, arrived late having gotten lost (hey, these places are often out of the way), but arrived in time to stroll around, eat, dance, and witness some fun and games. "First there was the best tan line contest, then there was the best no tan line contest . . . then we wandered into the open but semi-secluded video room and watched the screen half the time and a woman sitting near us sucking her guy the other half of the time! It was lewd and outrageous to see this happen so casually in public! Then we moseyed over to a room where the couple had locked the door but purposely left the cut out window and blinds open. Watching them in action on the sex swing sent us over the top and we retreated to a private room, locked the door, closed the blinds, and went at it!"

Exhibitionism characterizes stage 4. Couples allow themselves to be viewed without the direct involvement of others. The barriers to involvement by others can be physical, nonverbal, or verbal. Walls, gestures, or words. The advantage to a public club is that discreet monitors or bouncers enforce the adage that "no means no" as a sacred rule never to be broken. Private parties have rules, too, but enforcement is a bit iffy, especially for single women.

Sid and Cris were relaxing with other couples in a club's sixty-person, "Roman style" hot tub. "I took Cris's hand and led her to the island pad mini lounge platform that rested in the middle of the voluptuous hot tub. She pushed my head down, and down on her I went. She came and I was hard so we started to have sex. Men and a couple of women gathered around. They inched closer. Cris was in ecstatic rapture so it was up to me to be a manager and multitask! I held up my hand definitively, said 'watch only', they did and I did the deed! It's not always easy to be watched and watch out for your partner!"

Stage 5 swinger play is commonly called "soft swing." This is generally considered to be anything from simple same room sex, to laying next to each other, bodies touching, to each couple fondling the other with no penetration permitted. Needless to say, when a couple hooks up with another couple these parameters need to be negotiated ahead of time. This is especially important if you are in a group room (which you should probably avoid anyway until you are very seasoned) as you will likely be approached by a multitude of couples and singles. Soft swinging is best for some because it involves many of the pleasures involved in swinging without the emotional and physical challenges faced when physical entry of or by another person occurs. It is the swinging stopping point for couples primarily interested in exhibitionism or voyeurism. If that is your turn on, why bother to go further?

Tara and Tristan had finished dinner at the swing club and were enjoying a drink at a cocktail table near the dance floor. Tristan had on the all black NYC club uniform while Tara wore a revealing outfit she *never* wore anywhere else. She was braless with a see-thru top and a denim mini skirt that seemed to stop just below her crotch. This alone sent Tristan into sexual seventh heaven. They were approached by Kara and Ryan who asked to join them. "We said 'sure,'" related Tara. "We had a chat for a while and then some slow music came on and Tristan asked me to dance. Our newfound friends joined us on the dance floor. Tristan had his hands all over me and I was heating up. He was even raising my mini when he knew Ryan could see. This sent tingles down my stomach and then I could feel myself getting very wet. When the next song started up it was also slow and we decided to switch partners. It was such a hot experience I thought I was going to come on the dance floor! Ryan was polite, but forward. His touch on my back confirmed what he knew that I was not wearing a bra. I think he wanted me to know that he knew and that was so hot. He pressed against me. Again, the pre-come tingles. He lightly touched my butt. Tingles galore."

"When the music ended we went back to our tables. They suggested that we go to a private room to play. Just the way they said it made me sure that they were more experienced and wanted a full swap. Tristan and I stuck to our pre-club agreement and said we were only okay with soft swing. They looked disappointed but wanted to play anyway. Indeed they kept to the agreement.

But just stripping next to them and then screwing with our bodies side by side gave me one of the best orgasms of my life! Afterward, we sat around and Kara and I actually talked about styles of shaving one's pussy! Bare, toupee, or landing strip? Meanwhile Tristan and Ryan were talking about the Yankees World Series hopes! We then hugged, exited, told the sheet change person that the room had been . . . uh . . . used, and went our separate ways!"

Stage 6 swinging is what is often called "full swing." Here couples switch partners and penetration takes place, almost always oral, but very frequently genital as well. If you just want to engage in oral sex you need to make that explicit as a boundary/limit prior to going back to a play room. The absence of an agreement as to what will happen is perhaps the most frequent cause of a bad swinging experience.

Chris and Amy first met Ari and Rebecca at the Desire resort near Cancun. Chris: "They sat next to us poolside in lounge chairs. We exchanged polite pleasantries which is actually quite surreal when everyone is naked! We were taken aback when Rebecca said there was an emergency call from the daycare center. I said quietly to Amy what a shame it was to have such kid responsibilities at Desire. When Rebecca came back a half an hour later she said everything was taken care of. Upon empathic inquiry I discovered that they owned a doggie daycare center! We all laughed uproariously. It was the start of a great friendship. They had never swung, but we had a good bit, so we mentored them along because they were interested in starting. Amy tutored Rebecca on genital shaving options . . . bare, toupee, or landing strip? She chose bare and the next day Ari took the initiative and came to the pool shaved clean himself!

A year or so passed and we were still mentoring them along and emailing all the time. We had no designs on them because we are not pushy and, well, they seemed so swinging virginal. Then one night at a swingers sex club we met up at, Ari comes out of the men's room and takes me aside and asks, 'Would you mind if I hit on Amy?' After I told him that it was fine by me, but it was up to her. Ge thanked me for the positive sentiment. I gave Amy the heads up but we did not think anything would happen that night . . . it all seemed kind of theoretical, if that makes any sense. Yet Amy was fine with it and I related that to Ari.

The four of us wandered around looking at the various theme rooms. Amy stepped into one and started going back and forth on the sex swing like she was in a playground. Ari closed the door behind the four of us, a move we all thought odd at first, but then we all got it. Ari moved over to Amy and began touching her. She was clearly interested. He had trouble getting hard at first, explaining that this was his first time with anyone other then his wife since they married twenty-five years ago. Eventually he got hard and Amy put the condom on and swing they did in the swinging swing!

Meanwhile, Rebecca and I were watching the action. She started to play with my dick, but I ignored it and stayed soft out of respect—you see, on a number of occasions Ari and Rebecca told us they would never swing in tandem, at the same time. Later I learned that Rebecca did want to go at it, and she and Ari had changed their mind on all that. Opportunity missed!"

This is an interesting situation that illustrates simultaneously great communication regarding one half of the couples and an unfortunate lack of communication regarding the other half.

Stage 7 swinging could be called open swinging. Here one member of the couple plays with others without their partner being present. It is almost like having an open marriage except the uninvolved partner is usually in the vicinity and is cognizant at all times about the goings on. It is potentially more challenging to a relationship then even stage 6 penetration swinging because it can easily lead to deceit and emotional attachments. These are the two great enemies of successful swinging.

Gault passed by the room with the door open. At this resort in Costa Rica people usually nap in the afternoon before the debauchery of the night. Gault's wife had woken up after her nap and wanted a cup of tea, which Gault trotted out for, giving him a chance to get his coffee as well. But . . . as he passed the open room door a couple was beginning to have sex. He paused, knowing they would want to be watched. They not only did, they invited him in to watch! He graciously said that he had to get the tea back to the room but profusely thanked them for the great offer.

Gault acted smartly because his half-hour or one-hour tryst would have angered his wife who wanted to play with him and not be left behind, least of all while dressing in her "slut ware" for the evening ahead and craving a caffeine hit to boot. He did later relate that had he to do it over again he would have called his wife down for tea and a "show!" He will never know if she would have complied or complained, clamoring for his company. Partners need to need to know *before* not *after a* stage 7 spouse plays with another, even if doing so is permitted in the relationship.

So swinging is not a singular experience. It has levels and degrees of involvement. Moreover, far from the "key swap" and horridly titled idea of "wife-swapping" of the '70s, women are equally, if not actually more, in charge of what happens and what doesn't.

So those are the seven stages of swinging. If you want to be sure to remember them so that you do not go beyond your agreements in a moment of lust use Imaginative Relaxation to memorise them and where you and your partner will stop. Put yourself into that relaxed reverie and recite them to yourself while reminding yourself to let them sink in.

Also, if you want to get a sense of whether the next highest stage is right for you you can also use IR for that. Just go into an IR trance and do the age progression spoken about in an earlier chapter. It will give you a gut sense of whether you should move forward to the next level or stay put for sanity.

Next we will talk more about what a sex resort is like and what to expect if you go.

CHAPTER 16

What is a Swingers Club
or Resort Like?

Most swingers clubs have a number of common characteristics. Each however has a unique emphasis and atmosphere all its own. This chapter will talk about the expectable and usual qualities of the average club or resort.

One thing that won't be discussed is "off premises" clubs or house parties. These are places where you meet people and then, if you wish, go back to a hotel room, house, or apartment. This type of adventure is not recommended for the new or even intermediate swinger. Why? Because once you leave a club atmosphere you also leave behind all the security staff and bouncers as well as all the rules they enforce. You are somewhat at the mercy of the couple or individual you picked up. While almost everyone in the lifestyle is polite and has integrity, there are always a few individuals that will break boundaries and rules and provide for an unpleasant experience.

So, too, with finding people online, without the security of a club you don't fully know whom you are dealing with. First impressions can be wrong and second impressions can be scary.

Clubs are often located in out of the way places where zoning boards and neighbors won't complain about property values plummeting. In the city, they are often located in marginal areas or corporate sections where nighttime activity is sparse. One of the nicer clubs is located in a new pristine building on the grounds of a weekday active scrap metal recycling plant! You pull in and you might be parking next to a chain linked fence with hubcaps for various model cars secured on a line on the fence. But herein lies the paradox . . . clubs in out of the way and funky places can exist without objection, but more importantly people can slip in and out with anonymity. Having your kinky activities unknown to the public at large is critical to most people.

Before going you will need to e mail or call the club for a reservation. You are then likely to be given a reservation number, which you should keep for entry. Directions are usually online or may be given to you over the phone to ensure discretion. Note that GPS guidance often leads you astray.

Upon arriving and parking you will go to the entrance where you will no doubt be warmly greeted. You will need your driver's license or other ID. Do not worry, you won't be "outed," these clubs only wish to ensure that everyone is of legal age and to know who is in their facility. At some clubs you may be asked if you are an officer of the law. Just answer, do not freak out, they are just seeking to avoid trouble. Occasionally single men who are new to the club may be briefly interviewed to ensure they are not creepy. No worries here, this is only to create and preserve a positive atmosphere. Remember that people don't know that you are an upstanding citizen of the land of kink!

Being new to the club or scene, you will most likely to be given a tour of the club by volunteer veterans. You won't want to miss this, nor can you. It is more or less essential. This tour will give you a full overview of the club and your options within.

You will most likely first see a bar area and almost assuredly a dance floor. A buffet of varying quality and size, often there along with tables and chairs. You will also see the various theme rooms, the number of which will vary club by club. Theme rooms may range from mundane hotel like rooms to a mock jail, a wild west cowboy room, a sex swing room, and so forth. Some rooms will have doors that close completely for privacy, some will have bottom half doors that can close, some might have chains you can string across, and some might have windows that you can leave open to be voyeured or closed for privacy. All these options are designed so that people can have the flow of traffic that they desire. An open door means that people will want to come in and ask to participate. A half closed door or chained door will indicate that people can watch but not come in. Despite the clues, folks are likely to ask if they can participate. It is your call and your call only as to what to allow. In urban clubs people are generally more assertive, even aggressive. Yet always remember that "NO" means "NO." That is a cardinal rule of clubs across the board. Consent is king. Consent is also queen.

On your tour you will also encounter one or more group or orgy rooms. Reports suggest that these actually seldom get used—it is more common for three or four couples to play in a large private or voyeur room. On occasions where they do get used, it seems to entail a woman who wishes to experience multiple partners under the watchful eye of a significant other.

Most clubs have multiple areas and/or multiple levels. During your tour you are probably going to see a jacuzzi or a hot tub on the main floor. These are of various sizes, ranging from pool size to baby pool size. Strip and get in and it is guaranteed that before long you will have company by your side. Just remember that "NO" means "NO" no matter who sidles up next to you.

Resorts for swingers are entirely different due to their spaciousness. For North Americans, there are a number of resorts to choose from. That last sentence should be qualified by saying that people come here from all over the world.

In Jamaica ,there is one main sex resort, the infamous Hedonism 2 or Hedo 2 or, in code, H2 (there never was a Hedonism 1!). In Mexico, there are a number of choices, with Desire being the oldest and best known. There is one in Costa Rica. Many more dot the globe.

For one couple it was experienced like this:

> *Sheri and Kyle were new to all this, simply walking to the nude beach at Hedonism 2, a sex resort most respectfully*

catering to all tastes, from the tame to the wild. As they walked past the large Jacuzzi the ebullient entertainment coordinator was announcing the next event in the "Sex Olympics."

"Women, switch partners if you like, go down on your chosen man and the one that stays underwater the longest is the winner!"

A women named Hannah won with 60+ seconds of underwater time. Quite impressive if you were ever to clock it.

Next came the needed and inevitable male version of this "Olympic" event. Andre announced sheepishly that he did not like being underwater. Like all things Hedo, this was accepted with understanding. However Mark, Andre's friend, chimed up and stepped in and upped the ante.

He stated that "Before any other guy surfaces I will make Andre's wife come!" Applause rang out and the challenge was on. Andre nodded in clear approval.

Kyle said to Sheri, who was like a deer in headlights, to watch the woman's hands and feet, to see if they curl, and her stomach to see if it ungulates, to see if she really comes. He told her to ignore her vocalizations and moans. Kyle apparently was quite the aficionado of orgasmic activity.

Moments later all three events erupted, though lewd vocalizations were also heard. No other man had surfaced. Mark and Andre's wife were awarded gold medals and everyone retired to the swim-up bar to toast the victors.

Kyle, overly pleased with himself, walked with Sheri down to the nude beach. On their beach chairs they soon began discussing if they would wander back up to the Jacuzzi to actually participate in the 2:00 p.m. "dirty dice" game . . .

Hedonism 2 is typical of that which you are likely to experience when at a "lifestyle" resort. You will first arrive at the airport in Montego Bay or perhaps Kingston. Then you will go to the special resort welcome center which is likely to serve you champagne while you wait to board your shuttle bus for the resort.

The ride to the resort is interesting as you usually get to see a lot of the local flavor. Bus drivers usually stop along the way at small mom and pop bars to allow you to take care of your biological needs, which might include a Red Stripe beer, some rum, or ganja.

Upon arrival at the resort you are most likely to be warmly welcomed with more champagne as you check in. Rooms are either located on the "prude" side(swimsuits needed, but cheaper rooms) or the "nude" side. If on the prude side you can always stroll over to the nude side and just remove your trunks when you cross over.

You will be given a tour of the whole facility. This will include the prude side pool, beach, and restaurants. There is also a clothing optional quad pool which is so named because it is surrounded on four sides by four three-story hotel rooms. All pools feature swim-up bars, which are often the center of sex play.

The nude side is understandably the center of most of the activity. This is what most people come for. Just the same, Hedo 2 can almost be considered more of an exhibitionist's paradise than a swinger's resort. Sure, partners are switching off at a playful rate but PDAs (public displays of affection) abound and are somewhat more common.

The nude side consists of a large pool and largish Jacuzzi, and a beach area. There are two places to eat, an open air Jamaican restaurant and the swim up bar which serves delicious fast food type of fare combined with local specialties. Everything is all-inclusive, you pay not a cent while you are at the resort.

It is somewhat odd that with so many options people at whatever level of swinging tend to follow the same routine! Most folks get up in time for the full and sumptuous breakfast buffet which ends around 10:30 a.m. There you see people worn out from the night before but pumping with adrenaline for the day to come.

People then tend to wander over to the pool or beach to lay out and flirt. Sometime in early afternoon entertainment coordinators (ECs) engage people in games such as the "Sex Olympics" or "Guess the Penis."

"They chose us because we were just wed, though we had been swingers for a while," said a surprisingly shy Maria. She was voluntarily blindfolded and then her husband and five other naked people were put in a lineup. Maria, using her hands only, was to identify her husbands member! As is invariably the case, the lineup included at least one outrageously hung male and a *women.* "It was hilarious as I felt the different people . . . when I got to the huge guy I knew it was NOT my husband! Then, I couldn't believe how long I searched for the dick on the woman! Everyone was in tears laughing!"

In late afternoon most people take a nap and ready themselves for the night's festivities. This usually involves women wearing what is positively and affectionately called "slut ware!" Slut ware includes everything from dresses that end just below the crotch (no panties) to utterly backless dresses (did I hear you think "no panties?") to totally see-through tops. Men tend to wear New York City club clothes, that is, black on black or perhaps denim and black. In part the dress depends on the type of theme for the night—on toga night you will find men and women roaming around as pseudo Romans. On Jamaica night Rasta wannabes are afoot.

Dinner is the first order of the evening, in one of the many restaurants. You have to have your genitals clad for this!

Before and after dinner many people sit at the bar and chat. Eventually most wander up to the piano Karaoke bar, which is way more fun than anti-karaoke folks can ever imagine.

After the karaoke bar, people tend to go to the disco from about 10:00 p.m. until 12:00 a.m. Much fun but not as much fun as their next stop on the Hedo 2 nighttime train ride.

The Hedo huge, all-night hot tub comes next, complete with naked people of all shapes, sizes, colors, and genders. It is like a sexual three-ring circus, with every act performed as desired, none that are not, and an audience for all. The swim-up bar stays open until 5:00 a.m.

and things tend to wind down as it closes up. It is described as somewhat surreal to still be cavorting in the hot tub as the sun rises!

Then a new day starts with the breakfast brunch being put out around 7:00 a.m. and ending around 10:30 a.m.

So basically the day is done in two shifts punctuated by a nap in between. Sleep nonetheless tends to be shortchanged. Heard by a client in the brunch line: "I'll sleep when I'm dead!" Hey, it's a tough job but somebody has to do it.

Whether in the clubs or at a sex resort, Imaginative Relaxation can help you decide which wild is good by you and which is not. It is an invaluable tool—one that can help you sort out mixed and confusing feelings. Simply go into your relaxation place, adopt a "wish come true" mind set, and fast forward to doing the act in question. Then assess how you feel afterward. Alternately, you can go back in time to when you did something similar and remember again how you felt afterward. Using IR will be a prized tool for deciding which debauchery you want to do and which you want to discard.

AFTERPLAY

CHAPTER 17

Getting Off

Y ou have learned more than you realized in reading this book. You have discovered:

- How love relates to lust and how lust relates to family.

- How to use the game changing tool of Imaginative Relaxation to make kinky decisions and then actually become a kinkster.

- How to put yourself in a suggestible state to make the above happen.

- Important rules and guidelines regarding swinging and kink.

- The various types of kink and the variations of swinging.

- How to know what you want to do and what your flavor is.

- How to rid yourself of unwanted and unneeded shame and guilt.

- Practical and specific procedures and action steps to engage in BDSM, Kink, Fetish, and Swinging.

- That doing the above will provide you with highly hedonistic happiness.

So to bring it all together in a way that is sustainable yet evolving, continue to practice the above over and over. The emphasis should become increasingly on action and sequential implementation as you monitor your and your partners well being.

In addition, you may want to read my other books. They will fill in gaps and broaden your learnings.

I am always available to answer questions. Simply email me to ask anything or to even simply share experiences. You can also email me to set up an individual or couple's sex coaching consultation. If you do that we will connect by FaceTime, Zoom, or simply phone. Of course, if you remain shy (nah, after this book?!?!) I can do consultations by email.

It has been great being a part of your sexual growth and development through the vehicle of this book. Be well, mate in the wild and fuck for fun!!!!

If you enjoyed this book please, please leave a 5 star review on Amazon or whatever platform you bought it from! This means a great deal to me and will also inform other potential readers as to what to expect from the book! Thank you!

GET YOUR KINK ON:

Dos and Don'ts of Sexual Exploration

Other books by Dr. J. H. Edgette:

The Handbook of Hypnotic Phenomena in
Psychotherapy (with J.S. Edgette)

Winning the Mind Game: Hypnosis and
Sport Psychology (with Tim Rowan)

Hypnotic Erotic: A Practitioners Guide
To Sexual Healing

Forthcoming from Dr. J. H. Edgette:

Hypnotic Erotic Mating In The Wild: A Workbook

Dr. J. H. Edgette is available for practitioner or client
consultation. To book an appointment e mail him at
john@edgettetherapy.com

Dr.J is also happy to answer any questions about
the book or the issues discussed therein. He would
also welcome all comments on this book. He can be
reached at the above e mail.

.

www.ingramcontent.com/pod-product-compliance
Lightning Source LLC
Chambersburg PA
CBHW050732030426
42336CB00012B/1519